Desire

Breakthroughs in Mimetic Theory

Edited by William A. Johnsen

Desire
Flaubert, Proust, Fitzgerald, Miller, Lana Del Rey

Per Bjørnar Grande

Michigan State University Press

East Lansing

This series is supported by Imitatio, a project of the Thiel Foundation.

♾ The paper used in this publication meets the minimum requirements
of ANSI/NISO Z39.48-1992 (R 1997) (Permanence of Paper).

Michigan State University Press
East Lansing, Michigan 48823-5245

LIBRARY OF CONGRESS CATALOGING-IN-PUBLICATION DATA
Names: Grande, Per (Per Bjørnar), 1959– author.
Title: Desire : Flaubert, Proust, Fitzgerald, Miller, Lana Del Rey / Per Bjørnar Grande.
Description: East Lansing : Michigan State University Press, [2020]
| Series: Breakthroughs in mimetic theory | Includes bibliographical references.
Identifiers: LCCN 2018035659| ISBN 9781611863215 (paperback : alk. paper)
| ISBN 9781609176006 (pdf) | ISBN 9781628953664 (epub) | ISBN 9781628963670 (kindle)
Subjects: LCSH: Desire in literature.
Classification: LCC PN56.D48 G73 2019 | DDC 809/.93353—dc23
LC record available at https://lccn.loc.gov/2018035659

Cover and book design by Erin Kirk New
Composition by Charlie Sharp, Sharp Designs, East Lansing, Michigan
Cover art © Ali Mazraie Shadi. All rights reserved.

g green
press
INITIATIVE

Michigan State University Press is a member of the Green Press Initiative and is
committed to developing and encouraging ecologically responsible publishing
practices. For more information about the Green Press Initiative and the use of
recycled paper in book publishing, please visit *www.greenpressinitiative.org*.

Visit Michigan State University Press at *www.msupress.org*

Contents

Preface

When I was a young master's student in Norway, my focus was on desire in Dostoevsky's novel *The Devils*. While analyzing the novel, I discovered that the drives of every character were inspired by the other characters. However, Stavrogin, often described as one of world literature's most evil and, at the same time, seductively charming characters, was usually considered to have no models. He was perceived to be fundamentally evil. I found that strange. After many months' work, I saw that Stavrogin was also driven by a mimetic model: his absent father—not unlike Hamlet.

At the time, I saw no great difference between Girard's and Freud's understandings of desire. Later, I realized that desire can take any form. Hegel related desire to acceptance, Nietzsche to power, and Freud to the erotic, while Girard's understanding of desire as being "according to the other's desire" frees desire from any preconceptions.

I considered this point of departure very liberating. Desire could actually take any form, inspired as it is by the other. Thus, desire according to the other's desire is also my starting point in this book on desire.

1

The Nature of Desire

Desiring this man's gift
and that man's scope
— T.S. Eliot

A common theme in films, novels, or plays is how desire
works in characters and how it creates and changes their
destinies. The ability of certain authors to address the
issue of desire has meant that literature in the avant-garde
genre excelled in depicting human relations up to about
the mid-twentieth century. Today, however, the great insights into the individual seem to be an integral element
in all of the humanities. Autonomy in desire is considered
less autonomous than previously, and imitation is viewed
as something that infiltrates all areas of life. The taboos

surrounding imitation seem to have vanished. There is no need, therefore, to go "underground" in order to depict the fundamental ways in which desire dominates our lives. This is, however, easier to see, or accept, in the Western world than elsewhere. In many parts of the world, art as such is still the privileged outlet for desires not yet accepted by society.

Mimetic Desire

In this book, the view taken of desire has been inspired by René Girard's work on mimetic desire. Desire is considered a response to the other's desire; we want to have what others have. Research shows that within minutes, newborn children begin to imitate gestures from their surroundings,[1] indicating that imitation is deeply situated in our biology. However, desire in mimetic theory is considered to be distinct from instincts, as it has no braking mechanism and occurs after the fulfillment of natural desires. The term "metaphysical desire" is used by Girard in order to distinguish between sensual desires and desires that continue long after having been in desire. The mediator can both receive and hinder desire so that one's desires are transformed into secondary and rival desires. Thus, by imitating through a mediator, instead of direct, object-related desire, the subject becomes entangled in the mediator's desire. Desires will then intensify and exacerbate each other and pave the way for intense rivalry. As long as the subject and mediator desire through each other, their desires will become more and more symmetrical.

The romantic understanding of desire is that it is original and individual. If desire were based on the object alone, it would be based on a spontaneous attraction toward different objects, such as money, houses, and cars. In contrast to this view, Girard claims that desire is not spontaneous, individual, or primarily generated by objects but is mediated through what other people desire. He maintains that there is no such thing as original desire, only mediated desire. Thus, desire "is always reaching past its ostensible objects and finds little or no real satisfaction in them."[4] Desire in mimetic theory is not static and therefore cannot be fixed except in stages. The stages of desire are stages of decline, developing from a fascination with the rival to the final stage of being possessed by the same rival, and they can be explained in terms of the increasing intensity of the imitation of the other, which gradually becomes more and more conflictual. There is a development from fascination to rivalry, to conflict, to hate, and eventually to madness/murder/suicide.[5] If there is a stage where desire is most poignant, it is clearly in the later stages, characterized by serious conflict, violence, and illness. Thus, desire must be linked to, and defined in relation to, these negative phenomena.

Desire has a tendency to lead to nothing or nothingness. This means that it has no substance. At the same time, however, desire is the force that has the greatest power in shaping individuals—and society as a whole. The deeper one penetrates into the process of desire, the more symbolic, blurred, and sterile the desired objects become in the mind of the subject. Moreover, the references to reality become more and more blurred. The process associated with the ongoing desire for pleasure results in pain, again and again. This is the process by which wounds result from acting on one's attraction.[6] In other words, it is the process of desiring through desirous models, which eventually leads to nothingness.

The content of desire is metaphysical, therefore, devoid of substance, despite having the most devastating consequences for individuals.

Ultimately, desire leaves people barren, filled with a nothingness that resembles death. This does not primarily refer to physical death, but to a spiritual death where all that really exists in the mind of the subject is the conflictual presence of the other. According to the logic of desire, the problem is the mediator or the model, but the model will, if the rivalry is heated, seldom respond to the model's wishes. In this gradual development toward a death-ridden existence, the desiring person does not understand that the problem is desire itself. When desire has the upper hand in human relations, it is always the desired and despised model who is the problem.

Rituals, Prohibitions, and Individual Desire

One of the first uses of the word "desire" was in the Ten Commandments. Thus, desire was initially associated with wanting something to which one is not entitled and that will do harm both to the individual and others if acted upon. The ninth and tenth commandments, in particular, function as prohibitions against desiring things belonging to the other. The prohibitions in the commandments provide a kind of a priori basis in the Judeo-Christian world for an understanding of desire.

Prohibitions related to desire, however, do not provide an explanation of the process of desire. They merely state that breaking the commandments means going against the will of God. Both the analysis of desire in mimetic theory and the negation of desire in the Ten Commandments are based on prohibitions.[7] However, in the Old Testament this is more a warning against desire than a description of the phenomenon. In contrast, in the New Testament an effort is made in the Epistle of James to provide a more elaborate description of desire. "But each person is tempted when he is lured and enticed by his own desire. Then desire when it has conceived gives birth to sin; and sin when it is full-grown brings forth death" (James 1:14–15).

In this passage, there is a process that progresses from individual desires, to submission to these desires, to sin, and finally to death.[8] It begins with desire for an object, followed by a rivalry for the object, then the desire to outdo the other, and eventually leads to death. Viewed from a Girardian perspective on desire, in which the essence of desire is described as a process, there is a development through several stages: fascination, identification, competition, rivalry, conflict, and violence.

Viewed from a wider cultural and historical perspective, I consider that desire took on a new form once societies were no longer regulated by the scapegoat mechanism.[9] Desire then came to function as an individual and advanced form of victimizing, often less physically violent. Desire was what ignited and motivated the expulsion of the victim. It has become a more refined and subtle influence on human interaction. The development, made possible by sacrifice, into hierarchical societies based on different forms of us and them, inside and outside, which does not necessarily involve physical violence, indicates what I would call a shift from instinctual desires to more mental desires.

Desire has developed by becoming more and more individual. The transition from ritual to individual desire refers to the most basic and most astonishing transition in our understanding of desire. This hypothesis allows us to understand the development from traditional/primitive societies to modern societies. In the process of reducing and ending violence, sacrificial mentalities clearly change and become more individual. James Alison's claim that "desire is the 'interdividual' living out of a sacrificial crisis without public resolution" seems to support this hypothesis,[10] viewing desire as a part of an individualization process in a postsacrificial society.

Desire, Motivation, and Passion

According to Girard, desire begins in rivalry for an object[11] and ends in a purely possessive attitude, where the object plays a minor role. One could therefore claim that desire is a distinctively human phenomenon that can develop when a certain threshold of imitation is transcended.[12] Passion, in my view, differs from desire, since passion can be seen to denote positive human urges, in situations where imitation does not become rivalistic, and does not lead to violence but to love instead. Using the term "passion" in the anthropo-religious sense to refer to positive desires prevents us from viewing desire as something purely negative, thereby preventing the word from becoming demonized, along with its effect on society.

Desire can, in its most common configuration, be understood as a drive, as a motivating factor. Motivation is mimetic, based on the other. Nevertheless, the term "motivation," in its current usage, is too seldom considered to be triggered by jealousy, hatred, and admiration for the other. The concept is too weak. Motivation, therefore, is not useful as a concept to understand the catastrophic effects of desire.

The Dynamism of Desire

Desire is dynamic and cannot be fixed except in stages. The novel, therefore, which often covers a lengthy time span, is a preferred tool for depicting desire in its totality. The stages of desire are stages of decline, from an initial fascination with the other to the final stages of being possessed by the other and imitating his or her destructive desires. This can be explained in terms of the increasing intensity of the imitation of the other, an intensity that gradually becomes more and more deadly. There is, therefore, a development from fascination to rivalry and hate, and eventually, in the most serious cases, to madness/murder/suicide. "Desire is what happens to human relationships when there is no longer any resolution through the victim, and consequently no form of polarization that is unanimous and can trigger such a resolution."[13]

In everyday language, the word "desire" is used to describe competition, vitality, and creativity, while the latter stages of desire are often ignored and given other names. Actually, the latter stages are only the fruits of desire. In this respect, I would suggest that one could describe both positive and negative desire as mimetic desire, while purely negative desire is either described as metaphysical desire or, simply, desire. In this book, desire is almost always used negatively, denoting the development of a competitive structure in society that eventually causes relationships to sour.

Desire is initially a weakness; it consists of an urge to acquire something that one thinks only others have. This, however, is not the main weakness; the main weakness is the notion that if the desiring subject could have what the other person seems to have, they will be fulfilled. In the act of desiring, the other's weakness is not taken into consideration, since desire blinds people to the underlying desires of desire. Thus, the subject always has the feeling that he is pushing against a wall. He or she does not consider the fact that the other either desires the same object, so the last thing he or she will do is let the subject have it; or the other will begin desiring what the subject desires in a rivalistic manner. In both cases, rivalry will have the upper hand, and the chances of achieving what one desires are minimal.

The main weakness associated with desire is the fact that humans are not only unable to achieve the goals set by desire, they also invert the goals into the opposite: "Modern people imagine that their discomfort and unease is a product of religious taboos, cultural prohibitions, even the legal forms of protection. They think that once this confinement is over, desire will be able to blossom forth."[14]

When reflecting in a desirous manner, one sees only the negative sides of all prohibitions. Seen from a desirous perspective, prohibitions only exist to hurt or inhibit the subject. Desire creates an anthropology of freedom that claims that if everyone achieves their heart's desire, everyone will be happy. However, the opposite is the case, and desire seems to lead to unhappiness. It breaks up relationships, and in extreme cases causes violence. Prohibitions, therefore, can be seen to have been established in order to avoid such disastrous consequences.

The Nothingness of Desire

Desire is nothing or, more precisely, leads to nothingness. It is nothing in that it has no substance. The deeper one penetrates into the process of desire, the more symbolic, blurred, and sterile the desired objects gradually become in the mind of the subject; the references to reality become more and more blurred.

Ultimately, desire has no substance at all and leads to a nothingness that resembles death. It does not primarily refer to physical death, but to a spiritual death in which all that really exists in the mind of the subject is conflict.

Within the logic of desire, the problem is the rival. In this gradual process toward a death-ridden existence, the subject does not understand that the problem is a desire that produces rivals. When desire has the upper hand in human relations, it is always the desired and despised model that is the problem. This is because the subject is unable to reveal his own desires.

Desire is, it seems, the force that makes the world go round and, in its negative manifestations, creates all kinds of victimizations. According to Girard, "it is the acute mimetic rivalry with the other that occurs in all the circumstances we call 'private,' ranging from eroticism to professional or intellectual ambition."[15] Desire is therefore something that is evident in all areas of modern life. The great paradox in life is that desire governs our search for love, and at the same time, it often becomes the factor that hinders love's full blossoming.

· · ·

In this book, desire is analyzed with reference to works by Flaubert, Proust, Fitzgerald, Miller, and Lana Del Rey. Valuable insight can be gained from Flaubert's *Madame Bovary* regarding how reading novels can create impossible desires and, as in Emma Bovary's case, a serious attempt to cross provincial barriers in order to experience life as depicted in fiction. By following the directions in which her desire takes her, the reader can see both the workings of desire and, ultimately, how it causes her life to end in tragedy.

In Proust's *In Search of Lost Time*, desire is in the process of breaking down moral conventions. Proust describes not only the breaking of moral codes, but also the snobbery that causes the subject to hide their desire for the other. The great paradox in *In Search of Lost Time* is evident in the "Time Regained" section/chapter, where the subject has exhausted all the strategies available in an effort to experience fulfillment. Life among the once avant-garde and elite circles of the Fauborg St. Honoré seems, in the end, barren, not because of any puritanical ideals but because of the devastating work of desire.

Fitzgerald's novel *The Great Gatsby* reveals how desire to repeat the past ends in frenzy. Jay Gatsby's desire for the perfect requires a loosening of traditional ethics. His desire to climb in society lures him to take short cuts. Fitzgerald reveals how the arrogance of people with old money involves violence toward the less fortunate, and how their desire to hinder anyone new from entering their sacred world of wealth and privileges also involves destruction.

In Miller's *Death of a Salesman*, desire is viewed in the light of a distorted version of the American dream, in which the desire to be well liked gradually makes the characters lose their grip on reality and hinders success. The development toward a family tragedy grows out of Willy Loman's desire to be successful and well liked and culminates in an intense rivalry between father and son. They become mimetic doubles due to Willy Loman's intense desire to turn Biff into a successful businessman, and despite the love and loyalty they feel toward each other, they undermine each other's chances for success.

In my interpretation of Lana Del Rey's songs, I depict how desire, often the main theme in rock and roll, and in all her songs, governs human relations. In Lana Del Rey's universe, there is a never-ending desire to be loved. Her songs reveal a most profound insight into the repetitive nature of desire and how desire for one's beloved is shaped in accordance with the great American style icons. Lana Del Rey is an artist who, in her postmodern attitude, reveals the repetitive nature of desire by showing how obstacles always seem to pop up—just when the pleasant shores of fulfillment come into view.

her innermost dreams, dreams of romantic love, luxury, and heroic deeds, which are beyond the reach of a farmer's daughter in rural Normandy. *Madame Bovary* is a modern novel in the sense that character plays no decisive role. Everything changes and shifts in tune with desire.[2]

In order to reveal desire, Flaubert, as a writer vacillating between romanticism and a realism in its making, creates a world where everything is strictly realistic and, at the same time, is heavily laden with symbolic meaning. Most of the symbols prefigure the death and decay caused by desire. According to Corrado Biazzo Curry, desire transforms realistic descriptions into disorderly descriptions and juxtapositions of images without causal relations.[3] Desire in the novel is such a dominant theme that the most everyday descriptions seem to lose their original meaning and relate to some kind of strong urge. From chapter 4 onward, the novel's perspective seems to be related to Emma's state of mind: for example, the flat fields stretching their great surface until they fade into the gloom of the sky represent the monotonous existence to which she finds herself condemned; the closed shutters indicate a gradual degeneration of her life; and the muddy waters represent sexuality and lost love, while pure water represents her romantic dreams.[4] Landscape takes on such a "desirous" form that it annihilates persons and events, referring to cosmic emptiness.

According to Tony Tanner, mist and water represent Emma's disintegration.[5] Landscape in *Madame Bovary* is generally coated in lust, longing, and despair. Like the landscape, her two homes, the one in Tostes and the one in Yonville-l'Abbaye, both reflect despair and boredom, and the cathedral in Rouen is described as a boudoir, revealing Léon's erotic desires. Color also plays an important role in representing desire. For example, Flaubert uses the word "bleuâtre" (bluish) over fifty times, most often to describe Emma's fictitious ideal of love. Hazel Barnes has reflected on Flaubert's frequent use of the word "vide" (empty), claiming that it is a part of a language tinged with desire. One can say that the symbols coincide with a certain death wish, a wish to vanish or be absorbed by a greater whole.[6]

Emma's dream of liberation tends to take erotic paths, since sex seems to be the only way in which she can realize her romantic dreams. Her dreams of freedom are captured in the image of her sitting by an open window, immersed in feelings of hopelessness and melancholy, as she looks longingly at some open space and wishes that she was somewhere else.[7] The erotic symbols, however, seem to relate most often to a lack of sexuality. When Charles begins to visit Emma at her home (Les Bertaux), the burned-out embers prefigure a marriage that holds only meager sexuality. Likewise, the burned wedding bouquet indicates her future unhappy marriage. In contrast, bright fires from an open fireplace, one of Flaubert's more cherished symbols, seem to indicate real sexual desire, as when Emma, in her bedroom, thinks of Léon.[8]

Religious symbols generally emphasize suffering and decay. For example, the plaster statue of a priest that falls off the carriage and smashes into a thousand pieces during their move from Tostes to Yonville indicates that they are moving toward a godless existence and, at the same time, foreshadows the disasters Emma and Charles are about to encounter.[9]

Yonville-l'Abbaye is a wasteland, a place devoid of character, where they produce the worst cheese in the area and where nothing seems to grow;[10] it becomes a symbol of

Emma's experience of emptiness and boredom. In addition, her life is cramped; her sitting room has a particularly low ceiling, indicative of a life without mobility.[11] The graves in this small town are steadily encroaching on the available space,[12] hinting at Emma's own tragic death. Thus, in relation to *Madame Bovary*, Proust's statement that there is not a single beautiful metaphor in all of Flaubert's writing must be seen in a context of desire turning everything into ruins.

Mingling of the Sacred and the Profane

Emma's initial problem, and basically the cause of her suffering, seems to stem from her confusion about what to desire. In the Ursuline convent, where she has been raised from the age of thirteen, she reads romantic novels, which lead her from pious ideals to romantic ideals as depicted in works of fiction. Her childhood tendency to merge religious and romantic feelings develops into a lifelong obsession, and part of her tragedy derives from her inability to distinguish between these emotions. The first reference to her religious life emphasizes an inclination toward religious extremism.

> Instead of following the mass, she would study,
> in her missal, the pious illustrations with their
> sky-blue borders, and she loved the sick lamb, the
> Sacred Heart pierced by sharp arrows, and poor
> Jesus, stumbling under the burden of his cross.
> She attempted mortification, to go a whole day
> without eating. She tried to think of some vow she
> might fulfil.[13]

Although Emma is quite sincere in her religious feelings, Flaubert indicates that there is also a certain playful aestheticism in her religious life.

> When she went to confession, she used to invent
> petty sins so as to stay there longer, kneeling in the
> darkness, her hands together and her face against
> the grille, listening to the murmuring of the priest.
> The analogies of betrothed, spouse, heavenly lover,

and eternal marriage that she heard repeatedly in sermons excited an unwonted tenderness deep in her soul.[14]

This passage also reveals that her attempts at the convent to bridge romantic and religious sentiments ultimately leave her unable to distinguish between them. In her fantasy mixture of the spiritual and the erotic, Jesus becomes a heavenly lover.[15] The blend of romanticism and Catholicism in Emma's life is never separated, although there is a certain development in the direction of a purely worldly love. A visible shift toward the romantic seems to happen when Emma is fifteen, at the end of her stay at the convent. She falls increasingly under the influence of an elderly spinster who stays in the convent for a week every month in order to mend the linen. This woman, who is a member of an ancient aristocratic family, tells the girls stories, passes on bits of news, and lends the older girls novels. The novels were

solely concerned with love affairs, lovers and their beloveds, damsels in distress swooning in secluded

summerhouses, postilions slain at every post-
ing-house, horses ridden to death on every page,
gloomy forests, wounded hearts, vows, sobs, tears
and kisses, gondolas by moonlight, nightingales
in woods, and "gentlemen" brave as lions, meek as
lambs, unbelievably virtuous, always immaculately
turned out, who weep buckets of tears.[16]

This exaggerated outline of the content of these books
highlights the mature Flaubert's ironic attitude toward romantic novels. However, this is precisely the kind of novel he
himself read and believed in as a child, and he even reread all
the books on Emma's reading list. This passage addresses the
issue of childhood influences, influences that shape Emma's
romantic inclinations to such a degree that ordinary life
must make her unhappy. *Madame Bovary* is, even more than
L'Éducation sentimentale (1869), a novel about the effects of
education and learning. Like Frédéric Moreau in *L'Éducation sentimentale*, Emma's spiritual longing focuses on the
higher life as depicted in romantic literature. The difference,
however, is that Frédéric only partly believes in the education

of the heart. His cynicism becomes a kind of shield against romantic myths. Emma, on the other hand, has no cynicism in which to filter her romantic feelings; she lives for the moment, is incapable of denying her impulses, and never considers the consequences of her unbridled desires. She is strong enough to change her life by means of her desires, while Frédéric is a passive slave to desire, incapable of making a mark on the environment. However, Emma must always reach a certain critical stage of unhappiness before desire is transformed into action.

Thus, any attempt to identify the source of Emma's unhappiness should begin with an examination of her childhood and later role models. First, it is important to bear in mind that Emma never seems to be able to distinguish between profane and religious love.[17] On the basis of a naïve blend of romantic and religious sentiments, Emma begins to rebel against convent life, a rebellion that is attributed to the nuns' excessive religious practice. They had "so deluged her with masses, retreats, novenas, and sermons, preached so well the veneration due to saints and martyrs, and given so much good advice about modesty of the body and salvation of the soul, that she did as horses do when reined in too tightly: she stopped dead and the bit slipped from her teeth."[18]

It seems that she even rebelled against the mysteries of the faith. So when her father, Monsieur Rouault, comes to fetch his sixteen-year-old daughter, both she and the nuns are relieved.

After her return home, Emma's life is governed by sentimental dreams of adventure, luxury, and noble feelings. The contrast between Emma's life as the daughter of a farmer and the luxurious lives of women in romantic novels creates a chasm in her soul and makes her discontented with life. Not long after returning to the farm, Emma begins to dislike rural life. She even misses the convent and thinks of her convent friends from more wealthy backgrounds who have already married rich and handsome men. She grows disillusioned and decides that she has nothing more to learn, nothing more to feel.[19]

In her first lengthy conversation with Charles, she tells him that she finds rural life tedious and yearns for life in a town,[20] which reveals that her unhappiness is not, initially, the result of an unhappy marriage. Her role as a depressed romantic in the heartland of Normandy provides her with few opportunities. Emma is, however, privileged with regard to the quality of her environment, to the extent of her education, which in addition to religious instruction includes dancing, geography, drawing, tapestry work, and the piano.[21] Nevertheless, her father, Père Rouault, is far from rich, and due to extravagance his fortune is diminishing year by year.[22] Like his daughter, he despises the hard labor that farming requires.

Both Emma and Père Rouault are prone to strong emotions. In addition, neither of them can manage their money, so both live beyond their means, becoming poorer by the day. The narrator, however, never explicitly highlights these common qualities, but only indicates them. According to Mary Orr, Emma's sentimental religiosity and depressions are, initially, a heritage from her father.[23]

Although Emma is bright, always the first to answer questions on religious themes (she has even won prizes for her abilities),[24] there is no opportunity for her to live the life she wants. Her father excuses Emma for not being of much use in the house and thinks that she has too good a mind for farming.[25] At the same time, he sees no use in having her at home. Initially, it is his greed that makes him choose Charles Bovary as a husband for his daughter. Although he considers Charles "a bit of a loser," he senses that Charles is a steady young man, educated and careful with money, and, most important of all, one who will not haggle too much over the dowry.[26]

In short, Emma's background, consisting of being a farmer's daughter with no wealth and seeing her father living beyond his means, helps turn her religious sentiments into worldly dreams of style and wealth.

Emma's Romantic Desires

What was there in Emma's education that turned her into a romantic? The official education at the Ursuline convent could hardly be called romantic, despite its slightly Platonic air. Nevertheless, Emma has a tendency to transform Catholic teachings into romanticism. Gradually, her religiosity seems to fade as she becomes increasingly preoccupied with an idea of a life of luxury and heroism. Just before she leaves the convent, all her ideals revolve around tragic or heroic characters, such as Héloïse, Bayard, Clémence Isaure, and Joan of Arc, or privileged women such as Agnès Sorel, the mistress of Charles VII, and La Belle Ferronière, the mistress of François I. The royals whom she especially admires are those who display a special penchant for cruelty, such as Louis XI, who is famous for his unscrupulous methods for retaining power, and Henry IV, who is famous for slaughtering the French Protestants (Huguenots). All Emma's heroes are people who are out of the ordinary, extreme, and dramatic, people whose lives least resemble the simple lifestyle in a village and small town in Normandy. Emma's ideals are evidence of a woman who is living a life dissociated with anything in her current environment. To understand such a chasm between dream and life, it is necessary to examine romantic ideology more closely.

According to Henri Peyre, the notion of a romantic and sensitive nature has always existed, characterized by features such as a predominance of passion over reason, an emphasis on the extraordinary, dissatisfaction with the present, and a delight in suffering.[27] In this respect, Emma is the quintessential romantic. Other characteristics of romanticism include a longing for death and a taste for the morbid.[28] Romanticism implies a feeling of ennui in relation to everyday life and the confines of rationality.[29] Emotion is set up against reason. Ideal love is praised, while the inability to love is a source of agony.[30] Romantic poems tend to delight in solitude and in the contemplation of moonlit nights, employing various metaphors to underline feeling, referring to natural elements such as the sea, trees, the sky, dramatic mountains, deserts, and sunsets. Romantics are often enthusiastic about the Middle Ages and take a keen interest in travel and exotic places.[31] The loss of oneself in something exotic is a typical feature of romanticism. In keeping with this, Emma thinks that she can achieve happiness as long as she can travel and discover new places. Paris, in particular, is the place where all her dreams are centered. Flaubert, however, does not grant her access to the capital of desire.

Seen from this perspective, Emma fits neatly into the category "romantic." An exception is her preference for novels instead of poetry. This preference is based on a novel's ability to stir her sensations and make her feel fear.[32] Moreover, her view of nature is basically unromantic and very typical of people who live in rural villages. In her first conversation with Charles, she admits that she longs to live in a town. "But she knew the country too well; she was too familiar with bleating sheep, with milking, with ploughing." Nevertheless, if nature could stir her emotions and benefit her personally, she would willingly adopt a romantic view of nature. "She loved the sea only for its storms, and the green grass only when it grew in patches among ruins."[33]

Her preoccupation with madness, another characteristic of the romantic period, is limited to a certain focus on her own melancholy. With regard to religion, she is also basically romantic in her emphasis on the emotional elements. However, Emma did not turn to pantheism, as quite a few nineteenth-century romantics did, giving up their traditional Christian beliefs in favor of a pantheistic belief in a God inherent in all creation.[34] Nor does she revel in the cult of Greek religion and ancient Greece, perhaps because she does not have that kind of academic education and because the French romantics never joined that movement.[35] Unlike the romantics, Emma does not venerate the barbaric and primitive.[36] However, her fascination with the superman, which is strong in romanticism,[37] is clearly one reason why she gradually comes to despise her husband.

Love for the Sake of Being in Love

Emma's tragedy is partly rooted in her belief in the myths of romantic literature. Her life, especially at first sight, seems to illustrate perfectly what Denis de Rougemont describes as "the passion-myth" in our lives. According to de Rougemont, the passion-myth has, like a cancer, worked its way into the human breast of every individual in the Western world and created a perverse concept of love. It magnifies and deifies unhappy, nonsensual love and is, according to de Rougemont, a love for nothingness, for death.[38] De Rougemont characterizes this love as narcissistic love, in which the lover's self-magnification is emphasized more than the relationship with the beloved.[39] The love that is represented in romance literature is a love gained through obstacles, or even a love of obstacles. Thus, if there were no obstacles, there would be no romantic love. So in reality there is no love, only love of obstacles. Within the masochistic realm of love of obstacles, there is a pathological fear of falling in love in a simple, straightforward manner.[40] According to de Rougemont, this myth was bound to change the Western attitude toward adultery, which he considers to be materialized in contempt for marriage.[41]

Turning to Madame Bovary, Emma's initial obstacle is the result of her dissatisfaction with rural life and longing for a life in style and luxury far beyond her reach. Looking at Emma's life from the perspective of obstacles, it may seem that Emma does not love her husband because he is no obstacle. Admittedly, Charles does not seem to understand her and is not able to provide her with a stylish life and great passion, but his status as village doctor lifts her status somewhat—despite her having got an admirable cultural education in a convent. The more Charles seems to admire and even worship Emma, the more she seems to detest him. Her hate is partly self-hate. Like her, Charles represents the vulgarity of village life. This is highlighted in the vivid contrasts in part 1, chapter 8, when they spend a weekend with the aristocracy of the region; the party at the chateau (La Vaubyessard) stands in striking contrast to their own wedding party.

Emma's dissatisfaction with her husband seems to derive from a number of sources. Although Père Rouault undoubtedly played a part in encouraging Emma's marriage to Charles, she was not forced. As Emma watches Donizetti's opera, *The Bride of Lammermoor*, at the Théâtre des Arts in Rouen, she admits to herself that she, in contrast to Lucie, the heroine in the play, was full of joy when she was newly married.[42] However, Emma soon becomes bored and feels confined. There is no hint that she is being mistreated. On the contrary, Charles is depicted as a caring and loving husband. Emma's dissatisfaction seems to arise from a certain vulgarity in his appearance and his lack of ambition.[43] This causes her to long for something else.

From the perspective of modern mainstream psychology, it is possible to, at least initially, view Emma's problem as psychological: Her mother died when she was a little girl, and she seems to have had an unhappy childhood, except during periods of exaltation. Just after the weekend at La Vaubyessard, before they move from Tostes to Yonville, Emma's state of boredom and melancholy become so serious that she may be considered clinically depressed, verging on madness.[44] However, there are too few textual examples of early mental problems to determine whether this was an issue. Instead, the textual emphasis lies on Emma's extraordinary capacity for imitation.

One may question whether Emma would have been so easily beguiled by the representations of the noble life in literature if she had not been so discontent. Her first encounter with the life she has read about and longed for for many years is at the weekend at La Vaubyessard where she and Charles are invited to a party at Marquis d'Andervilliers. Once she has been introduced to this life and been able to taste the refined atmosphere among the aristocracy, her preoccupation increases. Everything that she sees and experiences at La Vaubyessard becomes, for the rest of her life, a norm and ideal. For example, the fact that she vaguely remembers the Marquise calling some girl Berthe leads her to choose Berthe as a name for her own daughter.[45] Shortly after their return home from the weekend, Emma's dissatisfaction becomes so strong that she sinks into a state of depression. The brief glimpses into the world of style and refinement have made her daily life seem ten times worse than before. Her intensified discontent culminates in her sacking her maid and hiring a new one who is required to imitate the service etiquette practiced among the aristocracy.[46]

Emma projects her feelings of dissatisfaction onto Charles. One of the reasons why one looks down on Charles is because he is generally depicted through the eyes of Emma. Thus, Charles is depicted through the eyes of romantic desire. From other perspectives, a more balanced picture may be obtained: "His health was good, he looked well; his reputation was firmly established. The country folk were fond of him because he was not proud. He was affectionate with children, never went into a bar, and, indeed, inspired confidence by his morality."[47]

Viewing Charles from outside Emma's desire for success, he becomes one of the finest persons in the novel. According to Mary Orr, Charles Bovary is perhaps the character in the whole of Western literature who is most often misunderstood. He is often viewed as a servile idiot, while, according to the text, he is generous, hard-working, faithful, and dutiful. Orr goes so far as to say that his goodness, his selfless concern for others, his kind and respectful humanity, and his belief in the best of others makes him one of Flaubert's many saints.[48] He is a good father and is extremely loyal toward both his wives. The only hint of any moral fault in Charles is when he breaks the promise to his first wife to never again visit the farm where Emma lives. Charles represents the nonmasculine man without social ambitions. He is the only character in *Madame Bovary* who is content with life.[49] His lack of desire hinders him in becoming a stereotype, unlike the other men in Yonville. He also represents an absolute contrast to his own bragging and brutal father. Nevertheless, Charles is not capable of enhancing his career as a doctor and is slightly clumsy and lacking in imagination; seen through Emma's romantic lenses, these shortcomings constitute a deadly sin.

Emma is not interested in such a dull relationship. She dreams of seeing the name Bovary displayed at the booksellers, repeated in the newspapers, and known throughout

into manners, and became part of the common language.[54]

One of Emma's heroes is Clémence Isaure,[55] who in 1323 founded the first literary institution in the Western world (the Academy of the Floral Games, which revived a game of verses among troubadours). This linking of Emma's passion to troubadour's love makes de Rougemont's critique of the concept of love as elaborated by the Cathars relevant to her romantic legacy. Although Emma seems to develop a more refined literary taste after the weekend at La Vaubyessard, and she begins to read contemporary French novelists such as Sand, Sue, and even Balzac, who tends to fluctuate between romanticism and realism, her underlying motivation is to find "vicarious gratification for her secret desires."[56] With regard to literature, Emma is like Don Quixote, who, after having read too many books on chivalry, becomes mad in that he sees the world through the deeds of the knight Amadis of Gaul. Like Don Quixote, Emma's desires are mediated through the desires raised by fiction, and like Don Quixote, she is forbidden by her own family to read romantic novels for a period.[57] Although I don't believe that de Rougemont is entirely accurate in blaming Western moral decay on literature, since literature can, as René Girard has shown in *Deceit, Desire, and the Novel*, also reveal the illusions of the passion myth, romantic literature is clearly a source of great unhappiness for Emma. The question is whether literature is to blame. A certain desire seems to be a necessary prerequisite for such a reading as it means identifying with the hero however badly his or her deeds afflict the other. In a way, de Rougemont echoes the prosecutor Pinard, who, during the court case concerning whether *Madame Bovary* should be banned, claimed that the novel destroyed people's moral consciousness.[58]

From Ideas to Relationships

In order to go further in our investigation on how desire works in *Madame Bovary*, it is necessary to shift the focus from ideas to relationships, and to examine the relationships between the characters. I will therefore gradually leave de

Rougemont's idea-oriented analysis in order to focus on relationships more than ideas. This means transferring from the ideological realm to the mimetic, and from de Rougemont to Girard. Although offering an alternative understanding, Girard praises de Rougemont's theme of obstacles,[59] even saying that de Rougemont is one of the few thinkers gaining novelistic insight.[60]

Girard claims that de Rougemont has not only seen the significance of the obstacle but has also highlighted the double structure of desire: the same movement that makes us worship life actually hurls us into negation and (inner) death. According to Girard, this view of desire, in which negation of life is depicted as vitality, is de Rougemont's most masterful insight.[61] Girard goes on, however, to elaborate a more technical device to illustrate the way desire works, introducing the triangular structure of subject, object, and mediator. He gently criticizes de Rougemont for not perceiving the third party in the desire for obstacles.[62] According to Girard, de Rougemont has revealed the fundamental content of desire, but his analysis lacks structure. Desire for obstacles is, for de Rougemont, a subject–object relationship, and he sees the obstacle as something within the subject (hero). The possession of the object is hindered by the subject's own mind, by the deceitful ideas of love created by myths and heretical religion. As the obstacles are the result of heretical ideas, and not of something concrete and contemporary, de Rougemont is therefore not able to explain the mechanism that links myth to mind.

Mimetic Desire

Emma's desire is constantly mediated by romanticism, transforming it into what Girard calls metaphysical desire, an internal desire that has lost its natural object and instead is mediated by a secondary desire.[63] Internal desire, according to Girard, is a process where the mediator or model comes increasingly closer to the desiring subject. The subject's initial desire toward the object is redirected and gradually becomes governed by a model or a mediator. However, in due time the mediator's desires also get infected by the subject's desires and they become doubles. According to Girard there has been a development in society from external to internal desires.[64] When the subject's desire becomes more and more based on the desires of the mediator's desire, desire is in a process of becoming metaphysical, which means that desire gradually loses its original direction. In the process of moving from external to internal desires, the relationship toward one's model becomes more intimate, psychological, and conflictual, and the need to hide one's desires becomes more acute. "In our days its nature is hard to perceive because the most fervent imitation is the most vigorously denied."[65]

What characterizes both Emma and the novels she reads is an inability to understand that desire is something borrowed from the desire of the other and does not contain some kind of essence or originality. As a result, she refuses to see the repetitions in her life. The overall mimetic development in *Madame Bovary* goes from the real to the unreal. All relationships tend to move toward the unreal. Her blindness to the fact that her own desires are being created by the desire of the other is a result of her narcissism and prevents her from seeing her own clichés.[66]

Although Emma is strong in the sense that she dares

to live out her desires, she is passive in the initial stages of seduction. She does not act until she really believes that there is a way out of her unbearable situation, and then she acts without any sense of the consequences.

Emma's desires are constantly being mediated by romantic desires, desires that turn and twist her spontaneity and make her loathe her environment. Before arriving at Yonville, Emma's erotic desires have vacillated between lifeless romantic dreams, on the one hand, and resentment of her husband's spontaneous and uncomplicated expressions of love, on the other. In Yonville her desperation grows, and her romantic inclinations begin to materialize in real erotic relationships, although she is, initially, the passive partner in both her liaisons. Her feelings toward Léon are ignited the first evening at Yonville when she and Charles have a meal together with some of the locals at the Lion d'Or. Her rather innocent and platonic love for Léon begins when they converse about travels, sunsets, music, and romantic novels.[67] Their immediate feeling that they are soul mates derives from the feeling that they are different from and superior to the others in Yonville. This sense of superiority is partly the result of their "sentimental education," which they feel enables them to understand the finer and more cultivated sides of life. Sentimental or romantic education becomes a catalyst for difference, facilitating an escape from the dreariness of rural life. Sentimental education seems somewhat similar to today's notion of "cultural capital," in that it distinguishes certain individuals from the masses. However, both Emma and Léon reveal a rather shallow concept of culture, solely based on feeling.

The spark of love is ignited by romantic sentiments and gradually develops during Homais's evening gatherings, where Emma and Léon, instead of playing cards and dominos, look through Emma's fashion magazines or recite poems.[68] However, Léon's naïveté and timidity, his bourgeois loyalty to good behavior and his shyness, prevent him from acting in a definitive way. Their relationship becomes an aching and a longing, with Emma listening daily to his footsteps on the pavement.

Léon never suspected that, when he left her house in despair, she immediately rose and went to watch him walk down the street. She wanted to know about everything he did and everywhere he went. . . . Emma considered Homais's wife a most fortunate being, to sleep under the same roof as him . . . . But the more she became aware of her love, the more Emma repressed it, to keep it hidden, and also to weaken its hold. She would have liked Léon to guess her feelings, and she made up fantasies about coincidences and disasters that might precipitate a revelation.[69]

The decisive moment in Emma's feelings of love toward Léon is emphasized by its occurrence in a moment of acute dreariness, a winter Sunday in Normandy when Emma, Léon, Charles, and the Homais family are visiting a flax mill. On this outing, the contrast between Léon and Charles is highlighted. Emma suddenly turns her gaze from the white wintry sun to see Charles with his cap pulled down to his eyebrows; his thick lips are quivering, which makes him look stupid, and his coat seems to sum up all the banality of his being. Suddenly, Léon steps forward. For Emma, his good looks and cultivated presence establish a definitive difference between him and her husband.[70]

After this very shallow experience of difference, Emma suddenly begins to change her lifestyle,[71] choosing a religious life based on duty and resentment. There does not seem to be any other reason for this shift from romanticism to puritanism, other than her feeling of despair that her love for Léon is impossible.

> But she was filled with lusts, with rage, with hatred.
> That neatly pleated dress concealed a tempestuous
> heart, and those chaste lips uttered no word for her
> torment. . . . . And then the pride, the joy of telling
> herself: "I am a virtuous woman," and admiring
> herself, in her mirror, in attitudes of resignation,
> consoled her somewhat for the sacrifice she
> believed she was making.[72]

In this part of the novel, readers gain a marvelous insight into how resentment works, as Emma's meekness is revealed as a form of rebellion. Behind her new puritanism lies not much more than the admission of the impossibility of her dreams. In fact, "the mediocrity of her home provoked her to sumptuous fantasies, the caresses of her husband to adulterous desires. She would have liked Charles to beat her, so that she could more justifiably detest him, and seek her revenge."[73]

If Charles had shared the combative nature of Emma's desires, their marriage would immediately have developed into a sadomasochistic relationship built on the thwarted desire for the other's desire. However, Charles never joins in erotic games based on rivalry. Instead he adores Emma whatever happens. Instead of serious rivalry, which would have suited Emma's romantic temperament, her unfulfilled desires turn into rage, and her feelings of dissatisfaction gradually evolve into depression.

The real affair starts three years later when a more self-assured and cynical Léon, who has been living in Paris, returns to Rouen. By this time, Emma has already had an affair with Monsieur Rodolphe Boulanger de la Huchette, a wealthy landowner in Yonville, and is prepared for the physical side of a liaison. The affair between Emma and Léon, which takes place in Rouen, becomes an imitation of the romantic love with which Emma has fed her mind during the years of boredom. However, Emma has more scruples during this second encounter than during the first. The narrator reveals that the attraction and temptation is stronger this time (she has never thought any man as handsome as Léon) than it was when Rodolphe rather insensitively and brutally seduced her.[74]

Léon knows exactly how to undermine Emma's moral scruples. In order to persuade her to share a cab with him, he says that a cab ride with a man is not considered improper in Paris. "Everybody does it in Paris!" Emma, who, through fashion magazines, novels, and maps, has dreamed of a life in Paris's high society, is unable to resist such an argument. The cab ride becomes an aimless tour. It may remind the modern reader of a road movie where desires have run wild. There is a certain awkwardness, even brutality in the description of this seduction. The driver's extreme discomfort seems to reflect Emma's own discomfort, and Léon's repeated angry shouts directed at the driver emphasize a lack of joy and pleasure.[75] Moreover, the cab is compared to a tomb,[76] once again prefiguring Emma's tragic death caused by desire.

claims that naturalistic sensuality is by nature the same as romance-desires, only sublimated to fit into an animalistic ideal. He seems to consider animalistic ideals to be as illusory as romantic ideals. It represents the same aspiration for the sublime, but viewed from the animal side.[80] According to de Rougemont, these animalistic ideals have been internalized and become a part of modern ideologies, as well as being prevalent in the mind of men, and have thereby become a glorification of instinct of the here below.[81] Both naturalistic ideology and romanticism operate with the notion that access to nature and love is straightforward and direct. Thus, this naturalistic approach is manifest as a belief in desire without a mediator. For example, in his attempt to seduce Emma, the figure of Rodolphe may, at first sight, resemble straightforward desire. However, it gradually becomes evident that everything is mediated by the characters' sentimental education. Both Leon's and Rodolphe's ideas of love consist of the same sentimental education as Emma's.

When Rodolphe contemplates seducing Emma, he evaluates her as he would a horse: lovely teeth, black eyes, neat feet.[82] These sensual elements, combined with the fact that there is the air of a Parisienne about her, makes her irresistible for both the outward romantic and inward naturalistic. In order to seduce her, Rodolphe needs to present himself and Emma as completely different from anyone else in Yonville; they are more stylish, their passions are stronger and more refined, and they belong on another plane of existence. Rodolphe reiterates exactly the same romantic ideals as Emma, but in an even more extreme form. In addition his romanticism, which hides his naturalism, is much more cynical than Emma's. The irony is that the reader sees Rodolphe in the context of the smelly, dirty, and deeply primitive agricultural surroundings, emphasizing his animalistic desires. Placing this seduction scene right in the middle of the novel seems to emphasize desire as the novel's main motif.[83]

When Rodolphe first seduces Emma, her reluctant manner is not simply coquettishness; she expresses genuine moral doubt. Immediately after having been seduced, however, Emma feels no remorse.

Then she recalled the heroines of novels she had read, and that poetic legion of adulteresses began

to sing in her memory with sisterly voices that held
her spellbound. She was actually becoming a living
part of her own fantasies, she was fulfilling the
long dream of her youth by seeing herself as one
of those passionate lovers she had deeply envied.
Besides, Emma felt a satisfying sense of revenge.
She had suffered enough, had she not! But now
her moment of triumph was here, and love, so long
repressed, flowed freely, in joyful effervescence.
She gloried in it, feeling no remorse, no anxiety, no
disquiet.[84]

Emma's feelings quickly go from being embarrassed and
frightened to feeling that at last her dreams have come true.
The mediation of desire through romance literature has
completely transformed her outlook, from initial uneasiness to fulfillment. Moreover, after the seduction, Emma
becomes the active party, so active and unreserved in her
search for love that it makes Rodolphe feel ill at ease and
frightened. The intensity of her desire causes their relationship to develop in a way that seems to be typical for all of

Flaubert's erotic relationships. According to Flaubert it is impossible for two people to love each other at the same time. Desire works in such a way that as love turns one party on, it simultaneously turns the other off.

Jealousy plays a fairly minor role in *Madame Bovary*. Instead of jealousy and rivalry between lovers, one affair follows after the other, and Charles, due to his trusting nature, never discovers these affairs while Emma is alive. Charles's jealousy flares suddenly after Emma's death when he first finds letters to her from Rodolphe and then those from Léon, and finally discovers a portrait of Rodolphe.[85] These findings tear Charles apart, physically and mentally. There is even a scene where he is on the verge of attacking Rodolphe. However, the scene culminates with him telling Rodolphe, twice, "I don't hold it against you," placing the blame on fate instead.[86] By not seeking revenge, Charles is ultimately able to quench the potential violence generated by Emma's infidelity. Nevertheless, the mingled jealousy and sorrow quickly ruin his life. Shortly after Emma's death, Charles also dies. The fact that the doctor finds nothing concrete wrong with Charles emphasizes the deadly effect of desire.[87]

Desire in *Madame Bovary* is a craving for the impossible, causing Emma to fight obstacles that are both illusory and unnecessary when viewed from outside the torments of desire. At the same time, the logic of mimetic desire enables the reader to decipher Emma's dilemma. For Emma, life becomes more and more tangled and twisted. As the end approaches, the narrator asks "why did life fall so short of her expectations, why did whatever she depended on turn instantly to dust beneath her hand?"[88]

In contemplating her own downfall, Emma seems able to see the paradoxes in life, in which there is always a negative side to the positive: "Everything was a lie. Every smile concealed a yawn of boredom, every joy a curse, every pleasure brought revulsion, and the sweetest kisses left upon your lips only a vain craving for a still more sublime delight."[89]

In her desperation, Emma perceives the downfall, but not the reasons for it. Both Emma and Charles blame fate for this downfall,[90] thereby displaying a lack of any great insight. Actually, all the characters in *Madame Bovary* lack depth of insight. All, with the exception of a little old woman named Cathrine Leroux who receives a medal for fifty-four years

However, if one restricts the analysis solely to the evolution of the novel, and does not consider Flaubert's letters, the novel's ideology seems to correspond to the ideas expressed by Homais, despite being such a limited and tiresome bourgeois pharmacist. Homais is a parrot of the ideals of the Enlightenment, in which rationality, science, and progress are highlighted and romantic feelings are discounted. His whole identity is based on critique of religion and expressing liberal values. Homais is an unstoppable networker, always sucking up to the right people, and somewhat of a charlatan in his work; nevertheless, he seems to represent a more successful alternative to romanticism. This rather one-sided interpretation of Homais, with its focus on his dullness and nonromantic temperament, which is evident in so many analyses of *Madame Bovary*, does not correspond well with the text, especially if one restricts the analysis to the development of the story: Emma falls into debt, Homais becomes wealthy; Emma's reputation is lost, while Homais becomes relatively famous. It seems as if the novel parts from any preconceived ideology. In fact, Homais's success seems to mark the novel's conclusion, and everything associated reputation and success. From her perspective of masculine survival and success, desire is motivated by a "more" in life and everything centers around the need to outdo others and victimize anyone who does not desire or strive for this "more." Charles becomes a prime scapegoat in the realm of masculinity due to his submissive attitude, respect for women, and lack of ambition.[93] In this context of male rivalry, where reputation and success are all, and where women are brutally subordinated, the worst characters become the most successful. The worst of these male figures seem to be Charles's father and Lheureux; the former is a brutal braggart, while the latter slowly kills Emma by tricking her into insurmountable debt. The flaw in Orr's overall interpretation, despite the precise analyses of the novel's characters, is the tendency to demonize everything masculine, thereby creating a dualism between masculinity and femininity, in which the former is all bad while the latter is all good. In this interpretation, Emma Bovary, although suppressed by masculine desire, is mostly bad because she acts in a typically masculine manner. Although there are, in relation to Flaubert's forced objectivity, many themes in the novel that lend themselves to analysis in the light of feminist theory, the theme of desire is so all-encompassing in its very nature that even the masculinity/femininity theme becomes secondary.

If the concluding chapters in *Madame Bovary* represent the author's own values, Flaubert certainly becomes, ideologically, less prophetic and more traditional. This is, however, in accordance with Flaubert's own defense of the novel, especially in the court case against him. In the court case he emphasizes that *Madame Bovary* is not a novel that propagates immorality but instead highlights the immorality of infidelity.[94] However, the loving way in which Emma is depicted indicates that the novel is first and foremost a tragedy, not a morality story. It is a tragedy devoid of any easy consolations, apart from the deeply moving scene at the end of the novel, in which at Emma's deathbed, the priest dips his right thumb in oil, touching the various parts of her body. First the eyes, then the nostrils, then the mouth, then the hands, and lastly the soles of her feet, as if all these sensual parts of her body have been reconciled to God.[95]

3
Proustian Desire

> But it is sometimes just at the moment when we
> think that everything is lost that the intimation
> arrives which may save us; one has knocked on the
> doors which lead nowhere, and then one stumbles
> without knowing it on the only door through
> which one can enter—which one might have
> sought in vain for a hundred years—and it opens
> on its own accord.
>
> —Marcel Proust, *In Search of Lost Time*

According to Germaine Brée, the deepest characteristic
of Marcel Proust's psyche was to create.[1] The desire to be
creative was no doubt essential to the young Proust. Yet,
if being creative as such had been his highest aim, Proust

would no doubt have tried to publish *Jean Santeuil*. There would seem to be a deeper, more profound drive behind the creation of *In Search of Lost Time*, a drive to depict the desires of man. The later Proust seems very far from a writer who typically savors images and characters. He appears to be uncomfortable with the genre of the novel as he constantly expands his narration into reflection, even into philosophy and psychology. His uneasiness about genre is, as I see it, the result of his trying to fulfill his obligation to describe the way desire works within the time span of a lifetime.[2] By beginning with Marcel's childhood and ending up at the gathering at the Guermantes where everyone has grown old, Proust wants to depict the total effect of the workings of desire. Space cannot fathom the way desire works; only time can reveal how desire changes, modifies, and destroys people. Also, time is essential in order to show how desire may be extinguished, how it can lose its grip on human beings and liberate them toward time regained.

The most characteristic understanding of Proustian desire is the way people try to hide their original desires and create other desires in order to preserve one's illusions about oneself. Desire is the force behind deceptive appearances. Snobbism should, in Proust's understanding, be seen to be governed by desire toward the other. Also erotic life is seen to be something fleeting and determined by models. The other main characteristic is the way Proust reveals how desire changes people's outlook on things. In society desire is the force behind the breaking down and building up of hierarchies. Also the constant changes of values are the act of desire. Desire becomes the main drive in establishing attitudes and world views. Proust seems to want to tell us that before there is politics, religion, and culture there is desire. And by the act of ridding oneself of metaphysical desire, Proust seems able to pave a way for depicting true art and experiencing a kind of resurrection, not unlike a Christian conversion.

Thus, Proust is not, as some critics claim, a writer governed by the norm of *l'art pour l'art*. He consistently tries to reveal the inner meaning of phenomena and constantly refers to ethical problems. The smells, the tastes, the forms are ways of recapturing and revealing the truth of (Marcel's) life. But at the same time, the desires he so vividly experiences

At the beginning of the novel, Aunt Léonie's house represents a bastion against the changing world. But gradually, with the aid of Marcel's naïve perception, we see the decomposition of yesterday's world taking place. The hierarchy, exemplified by the relationship of inequality between Léonie and the maid Françoise, is a relationship built upon external desires such as money, care, and so on. There is no threatening rivalry, no desire in Françoise to reach the same social level as Léonie. She is content with the prestige she gains by working for Léonie. This medieval mentality of extreme loyalty to society, to the superiority of one's master or mistress, is gradually disturbed by the introduction of a more intense and individual desire. One example of a desire that, still weak in its manifestation, seems to question the externality of the desires regulating Combray society is Françoise's sudden objection to Léonie giving money to a poor guest called Eulalie who comes every Sunday.[5] She objects to Léonie giving money to poor people, while she would have accepted her giving gifts to people of great wealth, the narrator tells us.[6] Proust reveals this objection as Françoise's rivalry with Eulalie. The internalization of this rivalry with the hated Eulalie is not, however, intensely metaphysical as it involves mainly an element of rivalry over Léonie's money. Although Françoise's desires are basically external, there are, in incidents like this, certain indications of a more intense internal desire creeping into the mind of the Combray inhabitants.

Léonie's attempt to live antimimetically, shunning the interaction of everyday life, may be seen as her strategy of trying to avoid the daily doses of desire, even if the consequence is a most morbid interest in all kinds of external events. Léonie's craving for support in her illness becomes, despite its rather cerebral nature, a scapegoating of anyone who does not support her or her views.[7] The bedridden Léonie becomes a symbol of the death of the old world, the slow decomposition of a hierarchical world in which external desires are being gradually transformed by the intensity of new models. There is an evolution in *In Search of Lost Time*, from the world of Léonie's house and the people living in it, who live a life of traditional values controlled by external desire, to the intensely degraded life of Baron de Charlus during World War I, where every kind of hierarchy is threatened by desire. Thus the further a character is distanced from the norms and customs associated with Léonie's house, the more acute internal desire becomes.

The new kind of desire creeping into Combray society is described against the backdrop of old-fashioned snobbery. But snobbery in the late nineteenth century is no longer an uncomplicated matter where one can, from the perspective of a certain class background, behave in a superior manner. The middle-class Legrandin, for example, represents a person who tries to live according to modern, liberal norms while, at the same time, erecting ancient mental barriers between himself and others, based on individual hierarchy. Legrandin's veneration for the aristocracy is not medieval; it is modern. Legrandin's desire toward people of the aristocracy can only be evoked in a modern, postrevolutionary world, where the hierarchical boundaries have become fluid and uncertain. This modern attitude allows Legrandin's sister, Mme Cambremer, to marry into the aristocracy. But the conflicting desires of envy and admiration make Legrandin outwardly despise the aristocracy, calling snobbery the sin that cannot be forgiven,[8] while in actual fact he is totally spellbound by the aristocracy, thus making him avoid people from the middle class whenever someone from the aristocracy is present.[9] Legrandin's love-hate relationship toward the aristocracy is only possible because the model of desire (aristocracy) has come closer to him, and his desire to be their equal is, in a rapidly changing world, both illusory and yet not illusory. Legrandin's snobbery is modern snobbery in the sense that vocally he is democratic and politically correct, but behind this correctness he gives way to the most fervent desire toward the privileged, the upper classes. Legrandin also uses literature and art to both hide and flaunt his desires, using lofty, romantic vocabulary as a means of distancing himself from his fellow men. His act of not allowing Marcel and his grandmother to be invited to his sister's home is a subtle way of reverting to ancient, hierarchical codes, in order to fulfill his more internal desires of snobbery and exclusion.[10]

Triangular Desire in the Bedroom Scene

The desires in Marcel himself are also gradually transformed and intensified. The desire for his mother's kiss, which can so easily be taken as an illustration of a Freudian triangle, is not motivated by any hatred for his father (otherwise Marcel would behave like this every evening). Marcel is testing out the boundaries of his mother's love. Proust is giving an example of a child's transgression. This decisive moment, seen from the perspective of a child's experience of desire, actually consists, in Marcel's life, in a breaking down of the hierarchical and bourgeois world. In Marcel's family certain laws must be upheld, not least when there are visitors present. The intensity and transgressive nature of Marcel's behavior also indicates the crumbling of the hierarchical world between the child and the grown-up. There is something of a child's liberation in the intense decision not to go to sleep before he has received his mother's kiss. The intensification of desire means that children's desires are also legitimate and taken into consideration. This zest for affection is indicative of a more general collapse in hierarchies. The crumbling of hierarchies does not only indicate the elimination of the difference between the haves and the have nots, but also the collapse in the grown-ups' authority over the child. However, the scene's intensity must also be seen as the result of his father's paying no heed to principle.[11] The internality of the scene is caused by the fact that the son imitates his father's lack of respect for the laws governing nineteenth-century hierarchy. If Marcel had not sensed, in some way, that it was possible to break down these not so solid walls of authority, his desire would never have been so intense. This reveals the double function Proust gives to desire: it not only breaks down the laws of morality, it also breaks down the laws of authority. A fiercer rivalry between the subject and the law is evolving. The sacred law of society becomes the semisacred law of the model, who will gradually, in all areas of society, become someone who is challenged and rivaled. Proust seems to be attempting to reveal different kinds of imitative behavior, behavior that is not governed by the changes in mentality taking place in society, but where the desirous behavior itself is changing the mentality of society. In this respect

his own middle-class background; they encompass all classes, or anywhere where desire reveals something potent. The reaction among the bourgeoisie in Combray is to scapegoat Swann, mildly but in a consistent manner, by excluding his family from their homes. This attitude of self-preservation makes Marcel's grandmother ignore everything that points to the exceptional social position possessed by Swann.[14] And she is perhaps the least envious and most tolerant toward Swann. Marcel's family cannot bear to hear about Swann's worldly successes. Their way of avoiding the threat of evolving internal desires is to stop, or subdue, all conversation that could awaken desire. Proust reveals this as comedy as, for example, when the highly symbolic conversation of Marcel's aunts is intended as an indirect thanks regarding the bottles of wine that Swann had brought as a present. The sterility of the conversation, where the desire to give thanks is hidden in subtle phrases, is revealed by the fact that it only has a puzzling effect on Swann.[15] Likewise, the general conversation in Marcel's family reveals the lifeless formality of ancient ways of conversing, at a time when the world is rapidly changing. Their stiffly upheld norms, their exclusion of the modern, must be seen as an attempt to rid themselves of all traces of desire.

Swann Is Marcel's Imitative Model

Swann also uses the forms of neutral, impersonal conversation in order to hide his latent desires, desires that threaten to crop up when he acts spontaneously, by avoiding concrete topics or topics tinged with emotion. Swann's technique of emphasizing important words with irony is a sign of internal desire taking a hold on reality.[16] But although Swann is able, in conversation, to hide anything reminiscent of internal desire, his life is possessed by it. This dualism between words and acts, demonstrated by Swann and also, to a lesser degree, among other members of Combray society, is what Girard calls organic falsehood.[17] Swann's distant and consciously impersonal way of talking can be seen to be an attempt to preserve the world of external desire, to avoid passing on the germs of internal desire to Combray society. But Marcel has already been smitten by the desire for the world of the salons. Swan becomes Marcel's mimetic model, the ideal in which his desires to enter the world of aristocracy and refined culture are ignited.

Outside Combray, Swann is totally prey to internal desires. Behind Swann's formal language, the young Marcel senses a man of great passions, living a life of refined deception. And later in life, Marcel will imitate just the same kind of love relationship with Albertine as Swann with Odette. In a way Swann prefigures Marcel's development, his future lifestyle, his pains. He also becomes his spiritual leader, unconsciously guiding him toward the salon world of internal desire.

Swann represents the new world threatening to penetrate Combray. And because this new world is governed by desire, it has no conscious understanding of its own evolution. Swann has no wish to introduce Combray society to this new mentality, although he is totally in the hands of internal desires displayed in the worldly salons. (His formalistic conversation could actually be seen as an attempt to avoid it.) But Combray gradually begins to reveal, in a nascent state, all the features of the worldly salons.[18] Therefore the movement from Combray to Paris and the salons marks a continuity without any perceptible transitions. In my view, the opposition between external and internal desire marks no opposition between good and evil; it indicates no absolute separation; it is only a development toward more intense and individual desires, which, with a paradoxical logic, end up in a most rigid monotony.

In Swann, Proust seems to build up a mimetic ideal, a man of the world, given most of the attributes needed to succeed in the realm of desire. Only the fact that he is a Jew and not from the aristocracy diminishes his prestige to some extent. Swann gradually becomes Marcel's alter ego. Both are middle-class. They both live from their father's wealth, they are both aesthetes, and they both get entangled with an uneducated lover from the lower classes, who is unfaithful. Both their female lovers have a certain penchant for pleasure with their own sex, and they both experience devastating periods of jealousy. Both Marcel and Swann seem to waste their lives, never managing to accomplish any of their planned projects. They are both, at various times, totally engrossed in the world of the salons, a world where desires such as envy, jealousy and social success are at their most intense.

The symmetry between Marcel and Swann is so elegant and technically understated that as a reader, one has no feeling of any forced, form-driven mechanical symmetry. And because the description is based on mimesis and not identity, there is no forced psychology of doubles. One might wonder, however, if there is a kind of romantic desire in the way Proust describes Swann. From a superficial or external point of view it appears as though Proust endows Swann with all his sympathy and admiration. Swann is certainly Marcel's mimetic ideal, even if the age difference makes mimetic desire materialize on rather external terms. But the young Marcel is not blind to the fact that Swann is not able to relate in a personal manner, that he hides his feelings behind a formal manner, making conversation awkward.[19] There is also the description of Swann's mind going blank every time something occurs that forces him to question himself. From this point of view Swann is like Jean Santeuil, a relatively successful man in the realm of desire. But the disintegration of Swann's success in the world of desire makes him evolve as a person deceived by his wife, his child, and his aristocratic friends, turning him into somebody sympathetic, but also pathetic, in that all his desires are slowly inverted; at the end of the novel, when he is mortally ill, his only comfort is his beloved daughter who, after his death, also deceives him by changing her name (not by marriage), thereby causing his name to vanish entirely from the world.

In the scene where Marcel breaks the laws of self-discipline in order to obtain his mother's kiss, Swann is the guest who makes his mother stay up entertaining instead of giving her son the good-night kiss. A kind of triangular situation arises where Marcel is threatened by Swann, since his desire for his mother's attention is thwarted. The triangular situation is entirely external in the cases of Swann and Marcel's mother, as on their part no kind of rivalry is implied. But Swann becomes a (distant) obstacle to Marcel, showing how the triangular scheme ignites, not because of any Oedipal family structure, but whenever desire is obstructed. In this respect there is something of a latent rivalry in Marcel's relation to Swann. Swann is able to hinder his mother's affection; he is capable of making her neglect the sacred ritual of the good-night kiss. Because of this, Swann has a certain fascination for Marcel. Swann evolves, in the eyes of the young Marcel, as a secular god, able to make people desire his presence, and hindering others in fulfilling their desire.

In this context Swann's smallest comments are of extreme importance. When Swann mentions the beauty of Siena, Marcel immediately begins dreaming of traveling to Siena. And Marcel is so spellbound by Swann's description of the Romanesque church at Balbec that the real church turns out to be a total letdown. Swann thus introduces Marcel to metaphysical desire, making the world of art larger than life.

Marcel's preoccupation with Swann rises at times to high comedy, for example, when the young Marcel wants, more than anything else, to be as bald as Swann.[20] Other examples of Marcel's attempts to be like Swann are when he sits at the table pulling his nose and rubbing his eyes, trying to resemble Swann's foibles, and making Marcel's father exclaim that his son is an idiot.[21]

Marcel is highly relieved when he hears from his mother

that she had met Swann at a shop counter buying an umbrella. Apart from the all-encompassing interest Marcel takes in Swann's whereabouts, the prosaic act also makes Swann more of a human and less divine figure. "What a melancholy pleasure to know that Swann, that very afternoon, his supernatural form silhouetted against the crowd, had gone to buy an umbrella."[22]

His reaction illustrates how admiration contains competitive desires and that while admiring a person, we simultaneously feel satisfied when something lowers that person in our eyes. Admiration also contains the desire of envy, because we want to become what we admire, and when the person we admire falls or appears prosaic, we feel that we have come closer to what we admire. Hence Marcel's ecstatic relief when he is told about Swann buying an umbrella becomes understandable. The same reaction occurs when Marcel hears that Swann has been to the dentist. The deity actually goes to a dentist! Any indication of some kind of human weakness means the utmost relief for Marcel. Also in this passage about Swann going to the dentist, Proust emphasizes the sacredness with which Marcel regards Swann.

On other days we would go along the boulevards, and I would take up a position at the corner of the Rue Duphot, along which I had heard that Swann was often to be seen passing on his way to his dentist; and my imagination so far differentiated Gilberte's father from the rest of humanity, his presence in the midst of the real world introduced into it such an element of wonder, that even before we reached the Madeleine I would be trembling with emotion at the thought that I was approaching a street from which that supernatural apparition might at any moment burst upon me unawares.[23]

Like anyone captured by intense desire, Marcel thinks that his model exists on a completely different plane from himself, finding it strange that his mediocre family even knows Swann. This masochistic tendency, enhanced by the repetitions of desire, makes Marcel feel proud when Swann even so much as recognizes him when he comes to fetch Gilberte.

When Marcel tries to convey to Gilberte how highly he regards her parents, he encounters the anger of the Swann family. In a world where metaphysical desire is to the fore, the most damaging thing for the self is to proclaim its desires. Gilberte tells Marcel that her parents cannot stand him.[24] Swann has detected some strong desire in Marcel, which makes Swann despise the child, thinking he has a bad influence on his daughter. Swann, as a social climber, has no tolerance for someone desiring him, as he, like Legrandin, in reality has no strong self-esteem or any genuine pride in his own human qualities. As with any snob, there is the element of despising oneself, and of looking upon any person who desires oneself with disrespect and anger. When Gilberte tells Marcel that her parents cannot stand him, Marcel writes a sixteen-page letter,[25] driven by the most urgent desire to convince Swann of his qualities. Thus, he is bound to make Swann receive a most unfavorable impression of him. If Marcel had been older and not protected by their difference in age, such display of the most intimate desires could easily have lead to serious conflict—as Dostoevsky reveals in numerous scenes.

Desire toward Gilberte

Gradually, when Marcel begins to play with Gilberte in the Champs Élysées Park, the desire Marcel feels toward Swann is projected onto Gilberte, showing that his desires are not directed toward any specific human qualities, but toward desire itself, or toward that which is desirable. After a short interval of playing with her in the Champs Élysées Park, the whole world for him revolves around Gilberte. A day when Gilberte is not there is a day without meaning. And the desires that the young Marcel shows toward Gilberte are clearly more based on imitative desire than true sensual desires. The way in which Proust allows children (Marcel and Gilberte) to have the same kind of desires as grown-ups reveals the universality of these desires. There is, Girard claims, no break in continuity between the child and the snob. Both imply the desire according to the other.[27] Thus, desire according to Proust is one and the same; it only takes different forms.

Not even the child can escape the terror and entanglement of metaphysical desire. The relationship between Marcel and

Gilberte is not very different from Swann's relationship with Odette (apart from the sexual dimension). As Swann saw Odette through the eyes of Botticelli, so Marcel sees Gilberte through his fascination with Swann. Even before Marcel has met Gilberte, he sees her as the privileged girl who goes on cultural trips with Marcel's favorite author, the famous writer Bergotte. So when Marcel finally meets Gilberte, accidently, when with his family on a walking tour, his desires are so strong that he is capable only of making faces at her. His seeing Gilberte through the images of Swann and Bergotte makes her absolutely terrifying in her fascination,[28] as the little girl, through Marcel's mimetical fascination, comes to embody art, aesthetics, style, and elegant worldliness. Gilberte incarnates most of the things that Marcel desires. Thus, when they meet in the Champs Élysées Park, there is, on Marcel's side, not the least spontaneity.

Proust depicts the relationship between Gilberte and Marcel as a relationship where Gilberte is totally in control. Gilberte has become both object and model in Marcel's initiation into the world of Swann. This insight into Gilberte's metaphysical role is indicated by the narrator. "Did I not then know that what I felt for her depended neither upon her actions nor upon my will."[29]

Their relationship is not conducted according to a natural, healthy feeling of getting on well together, of enjoying playing games. Gilberte represents Marcel's lifeline to the most sacred of existences. This prestigious role makes Marcel behave in the most servile manner toward Gilberte, feeling that her view of him represents the ultimate truth about his existence. Gilberte's claim that there are many other boys she prefers to Marcel is a result of both her childish honesty and roughness and Marcel's infatuation.[30] Marcel behaves in such a way that he is likely to be treated in a dismissive manner. The way Marcel begs her to tell him what he must do in order for her to like him again reveals a rather unusual desperation for a child, on the verge of masochism.[31] Marcel gives Gilberte the feeling that she must come and play with him every day. Therefore, she triumphantly, and a bit cruelly, announces the days when she will not come and play with him.[32] Their relationship already contains some of the same ingredients of exclusion, of master and slave, as in the relationship between Swann and Odette. Marcel naïvely imitates his alter ego Swann, while Gilberte unconsciously imitates her mother.

Creating a Private Symbolism

From this obsessive state of mind arises a private symbolism. The name of the street in which Swann and Gilberte live becomes sacred to Marcel, while Swann's name evokes the most vibrant feelings in him whenever it is uttered.[33] The personal symbolism is generated out of Marcel's desires, creating a world of subjectivity, devoid of anything common or general. His symbols cannot be shared by anyone or refer to anything outside his private desires. Thus, when removed from the context of his personal desires, Marcel's private symbolism reminds one of an artist who, in creating his own symbolic world, is incapable of communicating it to others. Marcel's father, whose insight into Marcel's private world is meager, reacts with the same irritation as a person who fails to understand anything of an artist's symbolic world.[34]

Swann in Love

While Marcel seems to have no impact on Swann's life whatsoever, Swann's drama is seen as a drama based on erotic desires. Swann is not only a womanizer; all his acts and motives are driven by his liaisons with different girls and ladies from all spheres of society. Swann is obsessed by women. He becomes friendly with a family because he is attracted, for example, by their cook, and unscrupulously breaks off contact with the same family when the liaison with the cook is over. Swann has no work, and his reputation as an aesthete rests more on the works of art he has bought than on any profound work he has written on the great masters. It is Swann who causes Marcel to become conscious of finding living models that resemble great works of art. The desire to make life match art has had a most profound impact on Swann's life since his desires toward Odette were aroused when he discovered that Odette's physical appearance bore a striking likeness to Jethro's daughter in Botticelli's painting of Moses's life.[35] Initially, however, Swann does not find Odette attractive. Her eyes are too big and her skin too pale. She is also quite banal and boring. But gradually she manages to seduce Swann by making him feel important and her companionship indispensable. There is, in fact, a motif of master and slave in their relationship, where Odette initially speaks of Swann as some kind of master, entirely superior to herself, but when he is caught up in his desires, the roles change dramatically: Swann becomes Odette's slave (due to his desire for her), and Odette becomes the master of rejection, using the triangular game, flirting with the aristocrat Forceville in order to provoke Swann's desperate jealousy.

Swann's seeing Odette in the light of Botticelli's great masterpiece actually begins after her attempt to seduce him and make him long for her. The identification with Jethro's daughter transforms Odette into a more desirable creature. Odette's offering sexual satisfaction, acting as slavishly dependent, and creating a triangular situation with Swann's discovery of her imitative likeness to one of Jethro's daughters are the ingredients needed to make Swann spellbound by Odette, who, from outside of the realm of desire, would otherwise seem vulgar and mediocre. Mimetic desire transforms Odette into a sacred goddess, an object upon whose life he is totally dependent. The development is entirely in accordance with the laws of desire. The repetition of small acts of rejection enhances Swann's jealousy to such a degree that he gradually believes he is going mad.

The relationship between Odette and Swann is a study in the laws of desire, where the most desirous becomes the slave of the least desirous. Odette knows perfectly well that she has no means of conquering Swann by any spontaneous attraction or by any natural or inner qualities. The only way she can win Swann's heart is by the aid of metaphysical desire, by making him fall prey to the repetitive sadomasochistic pattern of inclusion-rejection. The initial strategy is to humble herself, to be totally available, totally disposed to any of Swann's desires, so as to make him dependent on her affection and sexual willingness, then gradually to make the availability a little bit more difficult to attain, and then to gradually remove all the privileges, making him long for her affection and availability until he becomes so desperate that he will do anything, even marry her, to be liberated from the torment of his desire. The paradox, also shows the contingency of their affair. As the revelation of Odette's preoccupation with him is totally dependent on the time span, on the minutes to be filled with interesting conversation, before Mme Cottard alights from the omnibus at Rue Bonaparte, Proust also reveals the weak foundation of their love. The truth about Odette's feelings, which enables Swann to renew contact and later marry Odette, is actually founded on this chance meeting with Mme Cottard. But behind this happy encounter, giving Swann the courage to marry Odette, the same old pattern is repeated. Odette continues to be unfaithful, and Swann, having no real love for Odette, continues to waste his life in the aristocratic salons.

In the Odette–Swann relationship Proust depicts the development of desire based on exclusion. The outer circumstances change, while the inner processes stay the same. The laws of desire are at work, giving the repetitious monotony of infidelity and snobbery many different faces, but always amount to the same modifying and unhappy effect on each individual.

Desire Has Many Forms but Is Still One

Another important aspect of Proustian desire is that he sees the oneness or the unity of desire. Desire does not work differently in each individual. Proust, instead of primarily interpreting life from the viewpoint of space, sees his characters in *In Search of Lost Time* in relation to *time*, how desire modifies and changes them in time so that when the characters finally assemble at the home of the Prince de Guermantes, they have all become the victims of the harsh laws of desire. Desire is responsible for its own evolution and becomes a caricature of itself as it aggravates the symptoms.[39] The desire among the characters in *In Search of Lost Time* to be original and superior to others ends in the most banal uniformity.

> These key Proustian texts make the point that we are always dealing with the same structure—in other words, that desire is not really as interesting as it would like to make out. Far from being limitless in their possibilities, the surprises sprung by desire are always the same, always predictable and

mainly based, as far as I can see, on Proust's understanding of *borrowed desire*. Girard claims that Proustian desire is always a borrowed desire and that nowhere in *In Search of Lost Time* is it possible to detect a desire that feeds on itself.[42] There is nothing in *In Search of Lost Time* that corresponds to a solipsistic theory, he claims.[43] Everything is mimesis; even regained time is a representation of past experiences, a repetition of Marcel's previous experience, but now purified from the desires that blurred the original experience. Proustian desire is, in Girard's view, desire according to the other. But this is not the case, in fact, when Girard interprets Proust's conclusion. Proust, according to Girard, recaptures the past by recapturing the original impression beneath the opinions of others that hide it. This, according to my own impression, leaves the final insight to a rationality that is not mimetic, a discovery that actually presupposes an element of antimimetism. Although Proust, according to Girard, reveals that one has always copied others,[44] the final insight is based upon a freedom from copying. And Girard's advocacy of *In Search of Lost Time* as a paradigm of mimetic desire, where it is nowhere possible to detect a desire that feeds on itself,[45] does not allow for incidents in *In Search of Lost Time* where desire is described as biologically determined, for example, in the scene describing Saint-Loup's falsity regarding his homosexuality: "The falsehood consists for them in the fact that they do not want to admit to themselves that physical desire lies at the root of the sentiments to which they ascribe another origin."[46]

Here Proustian erotic desire is clearly more Freudian than Girardian, emphasizing physical or biological desires as decisive as regards to all other desires. In this statement the transformation of desire is caused by an inherent, physical desire that then produces compensatory desires.

According to Jean-Pierre Dupuy, Girard gradually understood mimetic desire more in biological terms.[47] Dupuy, partly by the aid of Proust,[48] deconstructs Girard's triangular scheme by claiming the fictitious reality of the object. Desire has no concrete reality as it is totally in the hands of the rival. The object therefore has no existence prior to desire. Jealousy is what transfigures the model into a rival. The rival becomes everything and is itself an illusion. The rival has become self-sufficient, and the triangular structure breaks down horror of Proustian love, according to Grimaldi, is a pain caused by absence, born out of unrest and disquiet. Love starts by a sudden desire to know a person whose mystery has become hidden by our indifference and stimulated by anxiety and our own failures.[52] Love actually feeds on its failures. To be satisfied means that love has come to an end and needs to be evoked by the pain caused by the lover becoming unavailable.

People are, according to Grimaldi, willing to suffer to such a degree because one is possessed by love. Love, therefore, is not real; it is brought about by our imagination. Desire is such that one wants nothing else than what one does not possess.[53] One's love life is therefore born of both anxiety and an obsession stemming from imagination.[54]

Grimaldi locates three theorems in Proust's experiences of love.

1. One loves only what one cannot own.
2. Suffering in love is caused by anxiety.
3. Desire ends when one feels safe from losing one's object of love.[55]

Grimaldi's understanding of Proustian love is clearly related to de Rougemont's understanding of passion kept alive by desiring obstructions, and instead of seeking the other's love, one desires the feeling of being in love. But for Grimaldi love is caused by an even more negative force than de Rougemont's desire for obstruction, as it is born out of pure anxiety. Both de Rougemont and Grimaldi, however, differ from Girard as they do not see love and desire as primarily caused by a mediator.

Dissolving of the Self

Mimesis, according to Proust, works in such a way that we do not know what comes from ourselves and what comes from the other.[56] For example, a writer imitates another writer and, by forgetting the imitative dimension, thinks he is a genius. And when desire blinds one to the mimetic dependence or influence, the mimetic reality is sublimated into an autonomous illusion. Desire makes a person blind to the fact that he or she is imitating. Desire, because it is dependent on mimesis, makes mimesis taboo. Desire wishes to quieten mimesis, make it uninteresting, common, and base, because desire cannot exist without new desires and, at the same time, cannot continue to enchant the ways of the world once it has been revealed as an act of imitation. As desire itself is mimetic, it does all that it can not to be revealed as desire. Proust's great discovery in *In Search of Lost Time* thus revolves around the role of the other toward the self.

This is exemplified in the way in which Marcel tries to become original, but his experience of being totally in the hands of others makes him gradually surrender to the fact that all his desires are borrowed. The characters' development in Dostoevsky's and Proust's novels are caused by a *transformation* of desire. This transformation, despite being a variation of desire, has a fundamental impact on a person's psychological disposition. Critics of *In Search of Lost Time* claim that almost all heterosexual characters turn out in the end to be homosexual and view this as something rather overdone.[57] But these shiftings can be seen, in fact, as an act of internal desire, of initially showing desire toward what is not desirable. In *In Search of Lost Time* Proust seems possessed by this revelatory insight into the falsity of desire, describing almost all his characters as being governed by the game of metaphysical desire, and thus professing false desires. This, however, does not mean that the characters need to be naturally or initially homosexual. There is also the possibility of interpreting this change in sexuality as a process of transforming desires, from the object to the models. In this respect sexuality can be seen as an example of how imitating a model is capable of transforming sexual desires, indicating that sexual life is not such a stable, biological phenomenon as usually conceived. Proust, being perhaps one of the least conventional thinkers of the nineteenth and twentieth centuries, reveals a much more fleeting image of erotic life than is usual, as erotic desires seem largely to be determined by others.

All the characters in *In Search of Lost Time*, except Marcel's grandmother, reveal, to various degrees, an obsession toward the other. The characters who present their individuality and eclecticism with the greatest fervor reveal, in the process of the novel, a morbid consciousness of others:

Legrandin, the despiser of snobs, is totally absorbed by people from the aristocracy; the arrogant Baron du Charlus is totally fixated on boys and men from the working class; Swann becomes possessed by Odette through the imitation of art.[58] Marcel himself goes through successive stages of deep fascination for Swann, the writer Bergotte, the actress La Berma, Gilberte, and Albertine. Even Marcel's father, behind his bourgeois ideals, reveals mimetic fascination for the diplomat M. Norpois. Thus, Proust tries to show how the characters are driven by imitative desire toward their respective mediators. These different configurations of mimesis reveal a varying degree of intensity and domination over the subject. Marcel's father is not possessed by Norpois; this imitation is more external than, for example, Marcel's desire for Albertine, which becomes absolutely self-effacing. However, Norpois's few positive words on literature are capable of changing Marcel's father's view of Marcel becoming an author.[59] In Proust's novel there is little room for any autonomous desire. Even Marcel's mother, who, to a lesser degree, has fallen prey to metaphysical desire, lives through the life of her husband, avoiding peering too deeply into

Proust's universe, less a way of changing personality than of a degrading existing personality, and the change will inevitably mean a change for the worse.

Dying from Desire

For Proust, revealing desire is the result of both being in the grip of desire and escaping its devastating effects. When overcome by desire it is difficult to describe desire without being captivated by the laws of desire, which inevitably means a certain propagation of desire. But the devastating effects of desire would seem to be the reason why the characters in *In Search of Lost Time* become caricatures. Samuel Beckett saw the real effect of Proust's insights when he claimed that the essence of *In Search of Lost Time* reveals that "wisdom does not consist in the satisfaction but in the ablation of desire."[62] Both Beckett and Girard claim that in order for one's desires to be revealed, they must in some way die. Proust's insight into the realm of desire is the process of allowing one's own desires to die in order to reach a truth concerning human beings. This death of desire marks the birth of *In Search of Lost Time*.

The death of desire comes about through a process of suffering. And this suffering is transformed into art. It is not the suffering that makes the art, but the act of ridding oneself of desire, which implies the necessity of suffering and which, paradoxically, opens the door to creativity, to past experiences and truth. The past that is captured is a former desire relived on contact with a relic of the past. Thus, memory is no longer poisoned and dominated by desire.[63] In memory there is no possessive desire.[64] This death is really a death toward life, as it opens the doors to the past. Such a structure is also present in *Jean Santeuil*. But despite such remembrance or recollection of the past in *Jean Santeuil* it is, nevertheless, a recollection of the past through desire. In order to write *In Search of Lost Time*, Proust had to abandon his self-legitimizing approach to life. Once he had lost the illusion of autonomous desire, Proust became capable of giving a precise account of his past, a past where desire is presented as a borrowed desire, a desire based upon the desire of the other. In memory profanes the original sacred objects and rituals. They are merely "hollow vessels into which we pour values which we create elsewhere."[66] This can initially seem to be the case. However, this view can only be upheld by reading *In Search of Lost Time* as totally governed by individual desire. Rather Proust seems to reveal desire in such a way that the narrator sees through his own delusions, and by doing this, religion slowly, by the decomposing of desire, becomes a truth in itself. Girard, in analyzing the process of dying from desire, claims that Proust underwent the same process as a Christian conversion.[67] He does not claim that Proust actually became a Christian. The claim refers rather to the process of dying from desire and regaining new life. In this respect, Proust, according to Girard, depicts the same process as a Christian conversion. "Proust espouses the Christian structure of redemption more perfectly than the carefully planned efforts of many conscientious Christian artists," he claims.[68] This process of dying from desire is not something that is completely unconscious in the text of *In Search of Lost Time* as the process of time regained is an allusion to John 12:24, where the seed must fall into the earth in order to bear fruit.[69]

From a novelist's point of view there is no knowledge, in the act of creating, of being before or ahead of desire. An understanding of desire can only be reached by retrospection and by becoming dead to its influences. Also, the critic is dependent on a similar development in order to understand desire. Being open to one's own biographical past seems to be a necessity for both novelists and critics.[70] This symmetry between novelist and critic as regards understanding desire springs from similar biographical sources: desire cannot be given a true structural description without experience of the paradoxical character of desire. An understanding of desire is in its essence something depicted from personal experience, of reflecting on why our beginnings never know our ends. This does not mean that one cannot speak of desires other than one's own desires. It means that depicting desire without profound experiences of how it evolves in one's own life means projecting desires onto everyone else in order to escape the truth about one's own desires.

However, the process of *falling from desire* can be located in various texts. Describing a process of falling from desire could be seen as far more fundamental than any change in ideas or lifestyles. A similar structure to Christian conversion is clearly present in Proust's work. Also present is a description of dying from the nastiness of the world. What is not present is any affirmative reference to a Christian belief. But although Proust does not refer to any renewal based on a belief in Christ, his descriptions of falling from desire certainly indicate some kind of renewal. A Christian understanding of dying from desires would mean that desires were transformed through an imitation of Christ. Proust does not positively link this dying from desire to the process of imitating Christ, even if the allusion to John 12:24 refers to Christ's death and resurrection.[71] This is, however, in the context, more a simile than a symbol. Neither does Christ nor a belief in Christ have any revealing or driving force in the development of any of Proust's characters, not even in the experience of regained time. But such a meticulous description of dying and renewal in *In Search of Lost Time* would, at the same time, from a commonsensical point of view, be unthinkable if it had had nothing to do with Proust's own suffering that had led to his dying from snobbish and self-legitimizing desires.

With regard to the structure of *In Search of Lost Time* as a whole, Proust actually goes further than merely creating a simile for Christian death and resurrection. There is also the suggestion of a life after death. Despite an agnostic spirit of doubt, there is some hope that the small seeds of meaning, of ethical responses and calling, may indicate a transcendence and may even be a sign of a greater resurrection. This is illustrated in a longer reflection on life after death.

Dead forever? Who can say? Neither spiritualism nor religion have proved the soul survives death, but everything happens in our life as if we came into it with an onus of obligations contracted in a previous life; nothing in the conditions of life on this earth made us believe ourselves required to do good, to be considerate, or even polite, or

to make the atheistic artist believe he was obliged
to make twenty fresh starts on a piece of work
that may excite admiration which will be of little
importance to his body when worms are eating it.
… All these obligations which do not have their
sanction in our present life seem to belong to a
different world, founded on goodness, scrupu-
lousness, sacrifice, a world entirely different from
this one, which we leave to be born on this earth,
before perhaps going back to live again under
those unknown laws which we have been obeying
because we were carrying their doctrines in us
without knowing who inplanted them, those laws
to which all profound intellectual work approxi-
mates and which are invisible only—if at all—to
fools. So the idea Bergotte was not dead for ever
is not improbable.[72]

Such a text could hardly have been written by an author
who was not considering a religious answer to life, despite
the fact that it does not refer to any religion in particular.

Thus, Proust's understanding of his own creation cannot be seen as something alien to a Christian understanding of resurrection, and therefore this creation, although not directly Christian, seems to be born of the same spiritual knowledge that we might call the fruits of Christian love.

Time Regained

In Search of Lost Time can be seen as a product of time regained, as involuntary memories seem to be the incitement for writing the novel. Before involuntary memory, the only thing Marcel remembers of the Combray of his childhood is the bedroom scene where he waits for his mother's goodnight kiss.[73] But preoccupation with involuntary memory was in fact something that Proust had also tried to incorporate into *Jean Santeuil*. In *Jean Santeuil* there is a description of involuntary memory evoked by the sound of a bell.[74] There is also a chapter titled "Impressions Regained," where certain smells bring back memories from the past, liberating the narrator from the present.[75] These passages in *Jean Santeuil*, however, are not in any way decisive as motivation for the writing of the novel or in revealing any hidden truth about his past. They are more like less significant reflections on time, evoking the past in the present.

Beckett lays great emphasis on involuntary memory (in *In Search of Lost Time*) as a decisive experience necessary for becoming an artist. But he does not interpret these involuntary experiences as a part of the liberation from desire.[76] Beckett regards involuntary memory from a more solipsistic point of view, enabling Proust to fulfill his talent as an artist and, at the same time, follow his calling. According to Beckett, Proust was a romantic in that he saw his project as a calling.[77] Time regained is not deliberately seen, by the author, as liberation from desire. And Beckett is probably right in regarding Proust as something of a romantic in his emphasis on affection (instead of intelligence), ideas (instead of concepts), and inspiration.[78] Beckett does not, however, seem to see any kind of antiromanticism in the way Proust reveals the universality of desire and, like Dante, shows the futility of that same desire,[79] revealing the baseness behind those people who, from a romantic point of view, are endowed with an aura of exclusivity and distinction.

Falling from desire is, in my view, the key that suddenly opens the door that Marcel has being trying to open, but that, because of various kinds of drives, has remained closed. Marcel, in the final volume of *In Search of Lost Time*, is a witness to a certain breakdown, both in his own life and in French and European culture caused partly by World War I. The inside reports from the secret Parisian brothels, including Baron de Charlus's masochistic need to be flogged, indicate the worst and final stages of metaphysical desire. Baron de Charlus's masochism is depicted as a direct response to his sadistic behavior in the salons, as an attempt to reach emotional equilibrium, but it is nothing more than a vacillation between one sort of violence and another.

After witnessing the breakdown of traditional values caused by the war and different kinds of individual desire, Marcel reaches a stage of resignation. His health falters and he enters a sanatorium outside Paris. The reader receives no information about what happens to Marcel during his years at the sanatorium, but we follow Marcel on his train journey back to Paris. In this part, Marcel is no longer the aesthete or the fashionable writer. He ponders over his lack of talent for literature.[80] The falsity of literature strikes him more painfully than ever. The joys of the mind, which Bergotte had claimed were the young Marcel's privilege, now seem a sterile lucidity.[81] Neither nature nor other people are capable any longer of providing him with inspiration. Marcel has reached a stage where he considers himself to be worthless.[82]

Proust describes Marcel in a state of fallen desires. Marcel has abandoned his aspirations to become a great author and great man of the world. He has witnessed, both individually and collectively, the most severe degradations, and the years at a sanatorium have not cured him,[83] only created a vacuum, an emptiness. This development, however, seems to be a necessary requirement in order to experience time regained. In the vein of a typical conversion, Marcel must first experience intense emptiness and despair in order for him to give up his worldly ambitions. But this void does not mark any renewal of life; it is only a *via negativa*, the preparation for time regained.

Despite this surrender of his worldly ambitions, he

accepts an invitation from the Prince de Guermantes, although without the frantic excitement of his youth. The reflections Marcel has in the aftermath of his experiencing numerous flashbacks of the past, caused by slipping on the cobbled street, wiping his mouth with a stiff napkin, finding a first edition of George Sand's *Françoise le Champi* (in the Guermantes' library), are based primarily on art. These experiences, however, reveal truths about one's past, which had been "smothered" because of vanity, passion, intellect, and habit.[84] But true art is, as the narrator tells us, quite simply, our lives.[85] This true art, however, is not our biography as such. Nor is it any kind of crude realism about our lives. Proust almost becomes a secular mystic when he attempts to describe what time regained is about. Time regained is about exploring the depths that lie unknown within us.[86] And in order to reveal such truth, one has to cancel out one's dearest illusions. These illusions are based on a superficial and illusory understanding of objectivity.[87] It is clear from these reflections that Proust clearly professes a very different view of art than that which is generally described as realism. He even, several times, dismisses realism,[88] although it more important and far superior to everybody else's. And, indeed, at times Proust himself does express this kind of arrogant, narrow-minded, and self-legitimizing attitude, scorning people devoid of artistic emotions, especially art lovers who themselves are incapable of expressing art.[90] There is a tendency in *In Search of Lost Time* to divinize art and, by so doing, to glorify the artist as someone aloof from the rest of humankind, following a sacred calling. This regained belief in art is also a part of time regained,[91] a part that clearly tends toward turning art into a new kind of religion.

It is difficult, however, to see certain parts of "Time Regained" as having been written from a humble and religiously motivated perspective. In fact there is a marked egoistical tendency in "Time Regained." The narrator who is humble, at one moment, is easily transformed, at another, into a rather narcissistic and hybrid narrator. In the scenes following a succession of involuntary experiences, the narrator begins to describe the people gathered at the Guermantes party as if he had entered a zoo. The deconstruction of the characters is not only a description of the transformation of desire, portraying the individuals more like animals than human beings; it also contains rather horrible descriptions of physical decay. If we were to strip Proust's excellence of language of its content, it might sound like a youth who despises old and ugly people. Proust's descriptions, which, on the one hand, present a marvelous climax of desires run wild, also constitute Proust's rather shallow and primitive revenge over the people he has gradually come to despise.

The conclusion of *In Search of Lost Time* reveals the truth both about the persons whom young Marcel has desired so desperately and about Marcel himself. The truth means unraveling the aura of godlikeness and discovering the true mediocrity of each divinity. This is only possible if the other is no longer seen through the deceptive glances of desire. Odette, due both to Marcel's fall from desire and to the modifying effects of her lifelong desire to succeed in society, has begun to look like a doll, a drunkard, a small child, a sterilized rose,[92] indicating an almost total loss of humanity. The Princess de Guermantes has absolutely nothing in common with the lady who had initially cast her spell on Marcel. This, of course, is partly due to the fact that Madame Verdurin has become the new Duchess de with any zest for righteousness or political equality. It is the work of desire.

The democratization of desire brings about a rather pathetic veneration for artists (to which Proust also clings) and turns Madame de Guermantes into a good friend of the actress Rachel who, at the beginning of the novel, was considered to be just as much a prostitute as an actress. And the Duke de Guermantes, who has been chasing young women throughout his entire life, ends up becoming a frantic and jealous lover of a senile and loveless Odette.

Time and Desire

The end of the novel focuses on the merciless workings of desire. Desire has transformed everyone and everything. It recalls a tempered version of Michelangelo's *The Last Judgment*. Everyone is, if not outwardly, then inwardly, suffering from the delusions caused by desire. Desire has emptied everyone, made them suffer and die inwardly, and then left them devoid of any attraction. The only thing left capable of making them desirable and attractive is snobbery, the last resort of desire. But desire has changed: the desire for titles is not, in postwar Paris, the main desire, while a new set of people are taking on the role of models to be desired.[94] Desire has swept mercilessly over the fashionable prewar set of the Faubourg Saint-Germain, gradually ruining their lives, leaving them full of desires but rather crippled as to their ability to arouse desire. This is the conclusion, taking the form of an inverted Nirvana. Time has not provoked any liberation or personal peace, only loss. Only for Marcel is the fall of desire a gain. It clarifies his true, desirous past and gives him a new outlook, paving the way, and bringing him the final inspiration to depict the true story of his life.

new opportunities, have inspired the whole set—Gatsby, Nick, Daisy and Tom Buchanan, and Jordan Baker—to move from the Midwest and West to the East. The East is the America of desire, of adventure, excitement, and freedom. Society is on the brink of great upheavals as the result of desire, although the West is still rather entrenched in its regularity and established patterns. Thus, in contrast to the East, the West represents a traditional society, where desire is kept under control.

World War I transformed the United States into a global political and financial power and marked the end of its isolationist policies and its sense of inferiority vis-à-vis Europe. By 1920, it is in a position of dominance, the most powerful nation in the world.[1] It had the capacity to impose its will on other nations. Given its position, America also became a leading cultural nation, creating what has come, partly through Fitzgerald's writings, to be called the Jazz Age. The 1920s in America was a time of great contrasts, as well as of changes; for example, on the one hand, there was a breakdown of traditional moral values and, on the other, a puritan revival that attempted to control this development by banning alcohol. This was also a time of great violence. Lynching reached a peak in the early twentieth century, and immigrant-dominated gangs roamed the big American cities.[2] Soldiers had returned from World War I, tired and confused after their nightmarish experiences, only to discover that there were no jobs. In this context of rootlessness, the dream of a new life seemed to flourish, creating the perfect setting to investigate how desire works.

Romanticism, Modernism, Mimetism, and the Breaking Down of Boundaries

Fitzgerald has produced some of the greatest descriptions of desire in the twentieth century. Typically, the characters in *The Great Gatsby* want to live with the illusion of spontaneous desire, and they believe that they are doing so. Fitzgerald is, as will become evident in the following discussion, one of the great explorers of metaphysical desire. He hardly ever describes healthy and natural erotic relations. The joy of sex is not evident in his work, and sensuous desire hardly seems to exist; everything is about rejection, social climbing, and a desire to be accepted.

In *The Great Gatsby*, Fitzgerald seems to shift between a romantic and a Romanesque understanding of desire. The enchantment lies initially in the romantic dream and its remoteness from reality.[3] Gatsby is clearly a romantic hero who tries to live his life on the basis of a single romantic longing. His dream is what James E. Miller Jr. calls *immature romanticism*,[4] as it belongs not to the present but to a past transfigured by imagined memory.

This examination of how desire works in *The Great Gatsby* begins with the objects described initially in order to attract the reader. Desire in *The Great Gatsby* is enhanced by references to technical innovations such as phones, cars, and airplanes. For example, the name Jordan Baker is constructed from two brands of car,[5] emphasizing Jordan's machinelike character. Desirable objects are in the hands of people with desires who live outside conventional morality, having loosened their sexual and marital constraints.

In *The Great Gatsby*, everything is speeding up, and even the natural world is called into question as people's vision of what is real and unreal in nature becomes blurred. Leaves on summer trees, for example, are growing the same way things grow in fast-forwarded movies.[6] People look perfect but slightly dehumanized, and their identities overlap. However, desire, which outwardly creates difference and individuality, is slowly turning everyone into clones, and even male and female are less distinguishable. For example, at the end of the novel, Nick is mistaken for Gatsby.[7] People are often described in fragments or gestures; a butler is reduced to a nose, Wolfsheim to nose and cufflinks.[8] The descriptions of Daisy and Jordan emphasize fashion, luxury, and leisure; for example, Jordan looks like an illustration in a (sports) magazine. Gatsby is likened to a machine that registers distant earthquakes,[9] thereby highlighting his sensitivity and indicating that he will be present wherever some sort of frenzy for the new is aroused. Gatsby is in control of that which is new, and he owns everything that is desirable. On the other hand, everything he owns and controls has a single purpose: to win back Daisy Buchanan.

Desire and the Narrator

Fitzgerald's literary style combines Romanticism with modernism. His prose is both poetic and psychological. Images and rhythms derived and developed from nineteenth-century poetry are combined with the precision, consciousness, and topical references that were, at the time, becoming the hallmark of modernist writing in both poetry and prose. Fitzgerald updates Romanticism for the twentieth century to meet the modernist demand for high-impact language; every sentence is packed with both poetry and meaning. At the same time, he challenges the conventional romantic opposition between technology and art, between machine and imagination.[10]

In *The Great Gatsby*, Fitzgerald writes from a distance that enables him to discover a more refined literary structure. There is no longer any authorial voice or narrator with full access to the characters. In his two previous novels, *This Side of Paradise* (1920) and *The Beautiful and Damned* (1922), Fitzgerald was playing out his own life, letting his protagonists wrestle with his own conflicting ideas regarding such philosophical perspectives as Nietzscheanism, naturalism, Romanticism, and Catholicism. The omniscient narrators in these novels are therefore constantly shifting perspectives in order to explore the author's ideological frustrations. In contrast, the story in *The Great Gatsby* is narrated by a character with limited access to the other characters. By making Nick Carraway the storyteller, Fitzgerald established the needed distance, especially between himself as the author and the protagonist. Nick dreams of absolute knowledge, but he is more and more inclined to see things from Gatsby's point of view. He vacillates between his father's bourgeois morality and Gatsby's romantic perspective. According to Gary J. Scrimgeour, Fitzgerald's first two novels reveal a fault that is common in the work of romantic writers, which is the inability to understand the true nature of the characters created.[11] In his early career as a novelist, Fitzgerald clearly had difficulty in distinguishing himself from his characters. One reason for the success of *The Great Gatsby* is precisely the fact that he managed to create characters who were not his alter egos.[12]

Nick's reflections are always tainted by his snobbish

and bourgeois background. Even though he comes from a privileged background, his attitude toward the wealthy elite is characterized by a certain aggression, as expressed in relation to Daisy, Tom, and Jordan. This aggression seems to be moral. At the same time, his descriptions of people of the working class (Myrtle and Mr. Wilson) reveal an attitude of mild disdain. Nor are the people from the lower middle-class, such as the McKees, exempt from his disdain, and his reflections on Gatsby are never completely free from this attitude.

While not a neutral observer, Nick is a relatively reliable observer. He is the only character in the novel who is low-key, observant, and perceptive enough to tell the story. The other characters are all prisoners of their own drives, uninterested in people other than those who can stir desire. Nick refers to himself as "slow-thinking and full of interior rules that act as brakes of my desires."[13] His curiosity, nearing voyeurism, and his inability to act upon his desires make him a perfect narrator. Although his moral principles seem to be basically unchanged throughout the book, his perspective gradually changes; he finds Gatsby acceptable after experiencing the violent lives of the very rich—even though he represents all that Nick had previously despised.

The novels and short stories that Fitzgerald wrote in the early 1920s tend to chronicle events that extend over several years. This lengthy time span was necessary in order to elaborate on the nature of desire. In contrast, the main story of *The Great Gatsby* is more condensed and takes place between early June and September 1922. However, these intense months are viewed against the backdrop of what happened five years earlier, in 1917, when Gatsby fell in love with Daisy. These two timelines come together when Gatsby arranges a surprise meeting with Daisy at Nick's humble and run-down cottage. In this extremely awkward, nervous, and initially uncomfortable meeting, the lovers are reunited after five years, and this inspires Gatsby to fulfill his great desire of recapturing the past as if nothing major has happened during the intervening years.

However, already at this reunion the impression is created that Gatsby is starting to lose his faith in his quest; doubts are surfacing.[14] It could hardly be attributed to suspense alone that he almost changes his mind and wishes he could cancel the tea party where he will finally meet Daisy again. This is one of the very few scenes in which the narrator actually enters into Gatsby's head, revealing Nick's growing identification with Gatsby.

Nick as a Go-Between

The first-person narrator, Nick, is constantly trying to become an omniscient narrator, understanding everything that is happening. In order to achieve this, he acts as a go-between. His initial reaction to the notion of infidelity is extremely puritan; when he hears that Tom has a lover, his instinctive impulse is to call the police. However, he soon moderates his moralism and becomes Gatsby's aid in the process of winning Daisy back. Nick is moral in a traditional sense, but he clearly does not consider the fact that Gatsby's liaison is not very different from Tom's.

The word "pander" is provocatively used in the closing chapter of the novel to describe the settler's optimism.[15] However, the word also sums up Nick's role in the affair between Daisy and Gatsby. Pander is derived from Pandarus, a character in Chaucer's *Troilus and Criseyde*, who acts as a go-between to foster the love affair between Criseyde and Troilus. Just like Pandarus, who advises Troilus in the wooing of Criseyde, Nick enables Gatsby to fulfill his love. Pander means to gratify or indulge an immoral or distasteful desire or habit.[16] In the original context in *The Great Gatsby*, "pander" is used in a lyrical description of America's past.[17] Thus, the fresh green breast of the new world appeals to various desires such as nostalgia for the past and optimism upon arrival in the new world. However, it also hints at a decadent modern America by evoking the crime scene where Myrtle's left breast swings lose like a flap, incapable of giving sexual pleasure.

Snobbism, Class, and Money

The concept of class has been a more important theme in Fitzgerald's novels than it has in the works of any other writer in the American tradition. While American writers such as Dos Passos, Faulkner, and Hemingway focus on World

War I from a soldier's perspective, Fitzgerald records the preparation for war in *The Beautiful and Damned*; and while the aftermath of war is evident in *The Great Gatsby*, it is seen from the perspective of Nick and Gatsby, as something distanced, from the past.

Fitzgerald's postwar darkness is merged with class distinctions. According to Robert Emmet Long, class and success are issues that Fitzgerald both delights in and, at the same time, perceives as darkly apocalyptic due to the upheaval of traditional social order.[18] The young Fitzgerald combines Romanticism with Nietzschean cynicism, gradually moving away from his Catholic roots. However, in the midst of his ideological struggle, there is a more acute struggle for prestige, and a desperate desire for acceptance. For Fitzgerald, this meant being accepted by the elite, meaning the rich and beautiful. It seems correct to say that the young Fitzgerald was a romantic caught in his own trap.[19] While Proust and Waugh were spellbound by the aristocracy, Fitzgerald is spellbound by the very rich. Hemingway had once said that the only difference between us and the rich is that the rich have more money; Fitzgerald, perhaps due to his family's mild slide from riches to rags, felt there was something rare, seductive, and mysterious about those who have great wealth.

In *The Great Gatsby* class consciousness is evident throughout the entire novel. Fitzgerald's marriage to Zelda Sayre, who belonged to a wealthy southern family, was only possible due to the great success, especially financially, of *This Side of Paradise*. Before his marriage to Zelda, Fitzgerald was denied the opportunity of marrying Ginevra King because her family was very wealthy.[20] Ginevra, like Daisy, embodied refined elegance rooted in wealth. Le Vot claims that Ginevra did not love any man; she was in love with love. Only recurrent crisis, dramatic quarrels, betrayals, and reconciliations could keep her restless heart ensnared. Against any man who thought he had won her over, she used jealousy artfully as a weapon, never losing control, maneuvering him into indefensible positions until his dignity was lost. Each of her affairs was a campaign in which she played at being conquered, giving a little to take a lot.[21] Ginevra later became the archetypal model in Fitzgerald's work for the unattainable and reckless woman men fall in love with.

Fitzgerald's father had told his young and ambitious son

the class border by becoming a soldier. As a soldier Gatsby is accepted into Daisy's upper-class society. The uniform becomes a shield against his humble background and allows him both to be someone else and to mingle with the rich.

Gatsby and Dexter, due to their modest backgrounds, are spellbound by wealth and money. For Gatsby, love becomes more important than the object of the love, revealing an advanced stage of delusion. Gatsby is in love with love, or the idea of love, which he thinks can bring some order into his confused and disordered life. There is scarcely a hint of real sensual love, either in Gatsby's relation to Daisy or Dexter's to Judy. In "Winter Dreams," Judy Jones is exciting and desirable, capable of making any man fall in love with her. She has understood that in order to always be the winner in mimetic desire, she has to be in a situation of continuous flirtation and give each man only a faint hope of success, never really giving in to anyone. However, her endless flirtations corrupt her, and in the end make her incapable of love. According to Roger Lewis, the wealth that surrounds her destroys at the same time as it creates.[22] The girls in Fitzgerald's world frequently reject the men, making them feel like they are cherry tree in bloom. The flowers on the trees look intensely beautiful, then suddenly the blossoms fall. Similarly, the characters seem only to be really alive in the few years when they are young, vital, and physically attractive, before desire overcomes them. In *The Great Gatsby*, the name Daisy must also be understood in this context as having a short life span. This "Spenglerian" cycle of springing to life and waning into a dull and meaningless existence where only nostalgia is left is a theme that Fitzgerald returns to numerous times, although never with the same intensity as in the 1920s.

These motifs of rejection, loveless love, and impossible relationships all come together in *The Great Gatsby*. In this novel Fitzgerald further heightens the desire by creating a hero who tries to enhance his social status by means of criminal activities and lies, thereby slightly changing Fitzgerald's cherished scene where the poor, handsome, honest, and vulnerable men are being rejected by wealthy women. Gatsby, in contrast to the typical honest protagonist, tells Nick that he belongs to an old family with old money. By claiming to be an Oxford man and the heir of a San Francisco family, he tries to elevate his past up to the level of Tom and

Daisy's, which, if possible, would grant him a similar social status to them.[24]

Gatsby's deficiency partly lies in his belief that one can create an earthly paradise. However, this belief is naïve, stupid, and defenseless when juxtaposed with the world of Tom and Daisy. Tom and Daisy are incapable of not showing their contempt for members of a lower class. Daisy despises West Egg, the home of the nouveau rich where Gatsby lives, which is described as "this unprecedented 'place' that Broadway had begotten upon a Long Island fishing village—appalled by its raw vigor."[25] This contempt, as well as the bond between her and Tom, is a matter of similar upbringing and education. The fact that Daisy, who represents old money, is appalled by West Egg foreshadows that her affair with Gatsby will be short lived. Her reaction to what she sees as a vulgar place and a rather vulgar party indicates that Gatsby will never succeed in his attempt to win her back and recapture the situation of five years earlier.

Although Gatsby is living a delusion, he perceives, in a flash, that Daisy's charm and sentiments are founded purely on money. "'Her voice is full of money,' he said suddenly.

That was it. I'd never understood before. It was full of money—that was the inexhaustible charm that rose and fell on it, the jingle of it, the cymbal's song of it. . . . High in a white palace the king's daughter, the golden girl."[26] Gatsby is so spellbound by money, luxury, and snobbism that the insight is merely an observation without any consequence, either in relation to Daisy or to his own lifestyle. However, this voice full of money has been modulated by good breeding, confidence, and good schooling, as well as by always having been loved,[27] things Gatsby has been deprived from and still yearns for. Not only is Daisy's voice full of money, the very language in which Gatsby seduces Daisy the second time is also commercial.[28]

When Tom reveals Gatsby's background and criminal activity in the scene at the Plaza suite, fright and revulsion are reflected in Daisy's expression, which Gatsby, blinded by his narcissism and Gnostic vision of life, is unable to see is a consequence of his exposure as a fraud.[29] In this scene, Nick is initially impressed by Gatsby's cleverness. Simultaneously he is baffled by the enormity of Gatsby's vision. Even after having been exposed, he clearly believes that he will still be able to change the past so that he and Daisy can start anew. Gatsby's rivalry is now so intense that the objects of both his love and his rivalry are totally blurred, and he seems to have reached the stage of madness at which there are no longer any objects present. Behind his Gnostic canopy, his self-understanding, his sense of being a Son of God, lies the most intense desire to be among the elect, with the same status as the superrich. At the end of the Plaza scene, everything is desire. The reader clearly sees that Gatsby's chances of realizing his dream are waning minute by minute, leaving only a pathetic shell that Tom does not consider a threat; he allows Gatsby to drive off with his wife, knowing that she will never leave him for a bootlegger and criminal.

After the car accident, when Gatsby is watching over Daisy outside Tom and Daisy's mansion, it is evident that desire has destroyed everything. Gatsby's vision seems weak and pathetic. As he leaves Gatsby to himself, Nick's thought is that Gatsby is waiting for nothing.[30] Daisy has gone back to Tom, Myrtle is dead, and, some hours later, Mr. Wilson will kill Gatsby and then himself. Desire for love, success, and acceptance has been growing and maturing, and ultimately the fact that when people of different classes mix, despite their outward differences, their desires are similar.

Gatsby cannot win Daisy with his money, but without it he would not stand a chance of taking her away from Tom. However, this chance is not real; despite his fantastic ability to hope and no matter how hard he tries, he cannot change his past, and he cannot change other people's pasts. Gatsby dreams of restoring order amid chaos, but his actions only create even more chaos.

In the novel, Gatsby is depicted as a superman based on his outward performance; he is the master of water, earth, and air, represented by boat, car, and plane; however, fire, the fourth element, symbolized by love, cannot be conquered.[33] As mentioned, this rejection by the rich is something Fitzgerald himself had experienced, although in a milder and less violent manner. Before his breakdown around 1934, Fitzgerald believed life was something that you dominated if you were any good.[34] Afterward, in his later years, he came to see that life dominates you. Gatsby, on the other hand, like so many great romantics, dies young and does not experience this gradual downfall.

Gatsby: A Hero and a Criminal

There is a certain mystery about how Fitzgerald has been able to make Gatsby into a hero. Gatsby is depicted as being boorish; he has no friends, only hangers-on. He is a roughneck, a fraud, and a criminal. He is frightening by his own lack of morals, and his lawless aestheticism is rather despicable. His taste is vulgar, his behavior ostentatious, his love adolescent, and his business dealings ruthless; and he is clearly dishonest on a personal level. He is interested in people only when he needs them to achieve his goals. His nice gestures stem from the fact that he does not want any trouble.[35] Most of what Gatsby is involved in is tinged with the most intense danger and desire; for example, bootlegging, fixing results in sporting events, and dealing with stolen bonds.

However, Fitzgerald does not describe in detail the shady and criminal sides of Gatsby's life; instead he hints, thereby holding the reader in suspense. The initial gossip is about his wealth, his parties, and his criminal past. When first introduced, Gatsby is described as a tanned, smartly dressed man of around thirty, with short hair, and exceedingly charming and discreet, with an aura of mystery.

According to André le Vot, Fitzgerald at the age of nine noted in his diary his suspicion that he was not his parent's son but a foundling of more exalted origins.[36] This theme is taken up in *The Great Gatsby* when Gatsby disowns his poor and very ordinary background and denies that his parents are his parents. Instead he looked upon himself as a Son of God.[37]

Nick thinks that Gatsby turned out all right in the end because, in contrast to the Buchanans and Jordan, he had a goal in life beyond personal satisfaction. However, a closer examination of Gatsby's Neoplatonic self-understanding and his urge to recapture past experiences reveals little beyond self-satisfaction. In a way, Gatsby represents the American dream. However, he is also dishonest and passive in relation to religion, and therefore fundamentally estranged from the ideals of the founding fathers.[38] The references to the founding fathers are therefore more nostalgic than real as their religious aims and ethos are inverted.

In *The Great Gatsby* religion or religious hope has

evaporated. Nevertheless, Gatsby himself is enormously hopeful. His ability to hope makes Nick admire him. But because there is such a gap between Gatsby's hope and the reality of his life, this novel is devoid of hope at the end; there is no fundamental change or breakthrough, in any of the characters' lives or world views. Desire in this illuminating novel has thoroughly released the characters from conventional Christian morals and, in so doing, exposed them to violence and death.

The Workings of Desire

Desire is initially a weakness; it consists of an urge to acquire something that one thinks others have. However, the core of desire lies in the notion that if one has what the other person seems to have, one will be fulfilled. In the act of desiring, the other person's weakness is not taken into consideration, since desire makes people blind to the underlying desires of desire. Therefore, the desiring subjects always have the feeling of being hindered in reaching their goal. They do not consider the fact that the other either desires the same object (and the last thing they will do is let the subject have it) or they will begin desiring the object of the subject's desire and compete with the subject for it. In both cases, rivalry will have the upper hand, and the chances of the subject achieving the desired object are minimal. Thus, the main weakness of desire is the fact that humans are not only unable to fulfill the goals set out by desire, their goals often end up the opposite of what one expected.

All the main characters in *The Great Gatsby* are liberal in the sense that they are willing to break the puritan code.[39] Tom and Daisy find the American dream in a dreamless, visionless complacency of mere matter. They represent substance without form.[40] Fitzgerald's early novels contained a breathless adoration of flapper heroines whose passionate kisses are tinged with frigidity and whose daring freedom masks an adolescent desire for reputation rather than the reality of experience.

When viewed from a romantic perspective, only the negative sides of prohibitions are evident. Seen from the point of view of desire, prohibitions only exist to hurt or modify the life of individuals. Desire creates an anthropology of freedom, a freedom that is premised on the notion that if everyone pursues their heart's desire, everyone will be happy. In deep contrast, Fitzgerald seems to indicate in this novel that desire threatens human relationships to such a degree that there is a need for prohibitions. Desire leads to conflict; it undermines relationships and, in extreme cases such as in *The Great Gatsby*, leads to murder, suicide, and madness.

Gatsby is incapable of compromising in relation to his inner vision. He is a Son of God, therefore he controls time.[41] At the end of the novel, the level of Gatsby's desire has reached such a pitch that he seems to have lost sight of his object (Daisy). In the scene where he is waiting around Tom's estate, there are indications of a development toward madness; his vision that he can repeat the past seems to have lost contact with any rational, worldly reality.

Gatsby creates his own rules and his own private morality that ultimately prove futile. Nick, however, affirms the value of Gatsby's failed dream. Since Nick is attracted to Gatsby, he is not able to lead the reader to the promised land, where desire is fully explored and revealed. At the end of the novel, he is still biased, although he has become less priggish and more broadminded.

In *The Great Gatsby* emptiness and moral indifference eventually lead to violence and death. Already in chapter 1, the brutality in Tom's behavior foreshadows death as a result of desire. At the same time, despite her wealth and beauty, Daisy makes the American dream look somewhat shallow and hollow. Her lack of contact with reality is exposed at one of Gatsby's parties when she describes a woman as gorgeous, while Nick describes the same woman as an orchid, scarcely human.[42] In the beginning of the novel, she suddenly suggests that a bird outside of the house is an owl, in order to hide the fact that Myrtle has been on the phone to Tom.[43] This is a reference to "Ode to a Nightingale," a poem about beauty, desire, and death, which in the novel is a symbol that echoes the hollow notes of Tom and Daisy's lost love.[44] Tom's infidelity makes her frivolity sterile and her sentimentality shimmy.

The characters' sense of uprootedness is partly a topological problem. Gatsby, Nick, Daisy, Tom, and Jordan are all from the West. One of the issues addressed in *The Great*

Gatsby is the conflict between the surviving puritan morality of the West and the postwar hedonism of the East. In a way, all of the main characters have become slightly decadent as a result of this move. Nick, however, can return to the West since he has not suffered the same moral degeneration as Tom, Daisy, and Jordan.[45]

Girardian Interpretations of *The Great Gatsby*

Two scholars have published articles on *The Great Gatsby* from a Girardian point of view. Both emphasize the scapegoat dimension in the novel. In "The Great Gatsby: Romance or Holocaust," Thomas J. Cousineau sees Gatsby as a classic scapegoat who, by his death, enables the other characters to continue living their violent and sacrificial lives. However, my main objection to Cousineau is the fact that he blames Nick for being the main scapegoater,[46] a reading that focuses on deceptive self-understanding instead of the desires that stem from violent action. Stephen L. Gardner, in "Democracy and Desire in *The Great Gatsby*," sees democracy basically being born by a heightened degree of mimetic desire, and thus seems to want to defend the old aristocratic world, the world of those born into old money, against the upcoming Romantic heroes who are about to arise from their poor backgrounds and threaten their privileges.[47] This kind of interpretation probably exposes a weakness in Girardian theory where the source for negative social upheaval is seen to be one-sidedly caused by the Romantic lie. This leads to a naïve understanding of a sensualistic and naturalistic oriented desire. The destructive acts such as in the violent workings of Tom Buchanan are, therefore, less exposed. Tom is, in both Gardner's and Cousineau's articles, treated incredibly mildly. It is telling that both tone down the episodes concerning the affair between Myrtle and Tom, and the episode at the Plaza Hotel where Tom's vulgar and dark social Darwinism is exposed. Thus the reader avoids seeing the close symmetry between Romantic and naturalistic desire, where Tom, in the words of Richard Lehan, seems to represent a naturalistic, physical force of the new America—"the America in which force is embodied in corporations and in money institutions, embodied in the

In Fitzgerald's work, there is often a connection between snobbism and racism. Fitzgerald's ambivalence is evident in Maury Noble's reflections on inferior races in *The Beautiful and Damned*.[49] However, such reflections appear to be less smart and more violent and despicable when Tom Buchanan claims "it's up to us, who are the dominant race to watch out or these others will have the control of things."[50] Tom tries to defend his position by referring to science or, more correctly, pseudo-science. Nick, however, seems to view Tom's racist remarks as an example of his limited intelligence and outmoded ideas rather than outright racism.[51] Even though Nick is the most considerate character in the novel and never directly scapegoats anyone, his attitude toward Jews and blacks is condescending, and he does not incorporate them in his American dream.

Gatsby's urge to rise in society leads to naïve imitation, sometimes making him look ridiculous. His house is modeled on a typical European style. It looks like a Hôtel de Ville from Normandy. It has a Gothic library, a Marie Antoinette music room, and a study that imitates the design of eighteenth-century Scottish architects Robert and James Adam.

Similarly, Myrtle's apartment in New York reflects her social ambitions; the dining room is vulgar and resembles French rococo paintings such as Fragonard's *The Swing*, alluding to the frivolity going on in the apartment.[52] Both Myrtle and Gatsby, despite the fact that they represent populist vitality, are romantics who lack taste and refinement. In contrast, Tom and Daisy have the taste that old money can buy, although Tom reveals a lack of taste by imitating the old colonizers' style in his choice of his riding clothes. He is actually a parody of an English country gentleman. Daisy is hollow and lacks integrity. The split in her is marked by an inconsistency of her looks. Sometimes her hair is blonde, sometimes dark.[53]

Lewis's comment that one cannot buy integrity or taste seems generally valid. However, taste is relative. Tom and Daisy's taste is a quality that is associated with their money and their backgrounds. The link between taste and integrity is no longer evident in either of them. Within a short time span, Gatsby has acquired the taste of the nouveau rich, and he is as lacking in integrity as Tom and Daisy, Jordan, Mr. Wilson, and Myrtle. Nick is the only person with any moral integrity, so despite their different backgrounds, he is able to like Gatsby. Otherwise, the lack of likeable characters in *The Great Gatsby* is remarkable. Only Michaelis, a young Greek who runs an all-night restaurant, is characterized in a really positive way.

The Victimizing Process

In *The Great Gatsby*, the seriously rich are both winners and villains. Nicolas Tredell, from a class perspective, sees Myrtle as the sacrificial victim whose dramatic death restores the equilibrium between Daisy and Tom. However, the victimizing game can be greatly expanded. Gatsby also becomes a victim of their thwarted desire, as does Pammy, Tom and Daisy's daughter. Tom also turns Mr. Wilson into a victim, thereby provoking him to victimize Gatsby. Gatsby's disruption of the Buchanan family, as if Daisy's marriage and child count for nothing, means that he is not an innocent victim. Jordan does not actively victimize anyone, as she is wrapped in an impenetrable narcissism.

However, her haughtiness and arrogance reflect a softer form of victimizing.

The victimization process may be viewed as the pulse that drives the plot in this novel. In most of the victimization scenes, the outcome is to Tom and Daisy's benefit. They are the novel's primary victimizers, sacrificing anyone in their vicinity who threatens their hollow and wasteful lives, even each other. The novel actually culminates in the car crash, where all previous desires suddenly come together in one event and constitute what may be considered a typical modern sacrificial scene in which violence is engendered indirectly and at random.

According to Tredell, romanticism in early twentieth-century America is bound up with capitalism, materialism, brutality, waste, selfishness, and infidelity.[54] He goes on to claim that romantic desire is insatiable and the desirability of the goal depends on its separation from the desiring subject. Once satiated, it ceases to be romantic desire.[55] Harold Bloom actually attributes Gatsby's greatness to the fact that there is no authentic object for his desire. Gatsby, Bloom claims, "is both subject and object of his own quest."[56]

Gatsby thinks he can realize his dreams by breaking the moral code. He clearly does not distinguish between money obtained by crime and money obtained by legal means. Tom and Daisy are also continually trespassing on moral ground, while Jordan lives her professional life by cheating.

Nick's attraction to Jordan is superficial throughout the novel. In their first encounter, she acts as if she is totally indifferent. She is boyish, fresh, and arrogant, which attracts Nick. She reminds him of a good illustration. Their affair seems half-hearted and lacks sensuality—a typical trait in Fitzgerald's work. However, Thomas A. Hanzo claims that Jordan's unconcern for any other standards beyond these of frank self-indulgence is evidence enough that the two became lovers.[57] Nick accuses Jordan of being a careless driver,[58] and she surprisingly responds with hedonistic honesty, saying that is why she chooses to associate with people who are not careless. In their last conversation, Jordan accuses Nick of the same carelessness that he has accused Tom and Daisy of, and at the end of the novel, Nick has come to the conclusion that Jordan has created her personality out of a series of successful gestures. Other than that her life is purposeless and empty.

him closer to Gatsby than he realizes. They both dream of a new and enchanted life in the East. Gatsby's schedule for self-improvement is in essence not very different from Nick's plans when purchasing books on banking.[61] They are both in search of the American dream, one by legal methods and the other by criminal means. Gatsby would probably not have been such a fascinating and mythological character if he had not been seen through Nick's eyes.

Nick is a reliable narrator insofar as he discards what is false, explodes wild rumors, and clears away misconceptions. His role resembles that of a detective. However, he is better at deciphering other people's motives than his own. He is clearly susceptible to the luxury of the Buchanans' or Gatsby's charm and attractive gestures. His relation to Jordan is, despite the physical attraction, tinged with irritation. Her arrogance, moral relativism, and carefree approach to life seem to both attract and repel Nick. However, due to the intensity of his desire, the reader never learns much about what really happens between the two.

A Novel on Idolatry

Read as a novel about idolatry, about how people become gods in one another's eyes, the Christian symbolism that runs through the chapters takes on new meaning. The biblically inspired prose indicates that, perhaps unconsciously, Fitzgerald is exploring a society in which idolatry has replaced Christian values. Thus, *The Great Gatsby* can be read allegorically as a story about the consequences of replacing a transcendent God with worldly gods. Gatsby is, one must remember, working in "his Father's business, the service of a vast, vulgar and meretricious beauty,"[62] alluding to Jesus as a twelve-year-old in the temple telling his parents "Wist ye not that I must be about my Father's business?"[63] The replacement of a transcendent God with a penetrating but noncaring god in the form of an enormous billboard of a staring occultist, Doctor T. J. Eckleburg, creates a wasteland where agape gives way to Eros. Desire for money, success, infidelity, and moderate violence has replaced traditional Christian virtues such as humility, patience, fidelity, and love of one's neighbor.

The religious overtones imply that Gatsby becomes a Son of God and Daisy his Virgin Mary. Unlike Jesus in the Gospels, his conception is a matter of vulgar and meretricious beauty. His church is a fake, in the shape of an absurd mansion, an imitation of a Hôtel de Ville in Normandy, and in this place of worship, instead of pilgrims praying, there is a constant flow of lonely, uprooted people chattering indecently late into the night, sipping cocktails and drinking champagne.

Gatsby is a Platonist insofar as he holds an image of himself as a Son of God. However, I would refine this perspective by claiming that he is actually a modern Gnostic; he is thrown out into this meaningless existence and has to fight his way through the emptiness clinging to a dream of recapturing the spark that was ignited five years ago in Louisville when he experienced a sacramental unity with his goddess. The kiss is compared to an incarnation, a blossoming.[64] Gatsby's dream of being able to stop time and nostalgically repeat certain moments of the past can be viewed as replacing the Christian hope and longing for heaven. Moreover, the aesthetic scene in which Gatsby shows Daisy his piles of beautiful shirts,[65] a sight that causes her to weep, is reminiscent of a religious sacrament.[66]

Gatsby is working his way from the material life, renouncing his parents because they are lost in the mire of matter, while he is saved by the exertion of great willpower, which enables him to recapture and prolong these moments of bliss. The madness of the whole project lies not in the attempt to repeat the past but in the attempt to repeat the past as if the circumstances have not changed. Such attempts are, in practice, impossible when one does not consider the changes. This seems, in the case of Gatsby, absolutely impossible. The fact that he keeps looking at Tom and Daisy's daughter with surprise, without having really believed in her existence,[67] reveals the madness of his plan. Gatsby is incapable of considering the five years that have passed. To Gatsby, the fact that Daisy has married and given birth to a daughter is only a preliminary hindrance. The urge to wipe out these five years is Gatsby's madness, revealing an advanced stage of narcissism.

Gatsby's Gnosticism, materialized as a modern version of Gnosticism, is reminiscent of the classic Gnostic world view in which the development is from the material to the psychic. However, the psychic in *The Great Gatsby* is a development toward a form of sterility in which desire creates various forms of psychic prisons.

Even though Gatsby has been able to acquire all the material goods that people usually dream of, these give him no real pleasure. Gatsby's sole pleasure lies in trying to win back Daisy in order to fulfill his dream of evoking the same deep feelings he had experienced five years earlier. Clearly, this sacred moment was, for Gatsby, a religious epiphany. The moment when he kisses Daisy for the first time, he sees, out of the corner of his eye, that the blocks of the sidewalk form a *ladder* that climbs to "a secret place above the trees."[68] The ladder alludes to Jacob's dream (Genesis 28:10–19) in which angels are revealed going up and down a ladder and the Lord is standing beside him in a place named *Beth-El* ("House of God").

Being a Son of God, Gatsby is linked to Gnostics such as Simon Magus and to later Gnostics who, according to Irenaeus, think they are spiritual by nature and do not have to live a moral life in order to be saved. As it is impossible for the earthly element to partake in salvation, spiritual man can "intemperately serve the lusts of the flesh and say that one renders flesh to the flesh and spirit to the spirit."[69]

While the Romantics extolled the glories of nature, the world represented in *The Great Gatsby* gradually changes into a ghostly world in which nature becomes something grotesque.[70] Nick speaks metaphorically of the earth lurching away from the sun.[71] The earth is described as stumbling inelegantly and erratically away from the sun, which indicates that the earth no longer has any real life source on which to grow. At the end of chapter 8, Nick tries to enter into Gatsby's haunted mind the day after the car accident; he tries to imagine how unreal Gatsby must find the new world into which he has been thrown so brutally. Nick describes the sunlight as raw, a rose as grotesque, and leaves as frightening,[72] as if experiencing a world that is material without being real.

The depreciation of nature, which Hans Jonas claims is a common trait in both Gnosticism and existentialism,[73] can, in *The Great Gatsby*, be the consequence of desire run wild. The last sentence in the novel, "so we beat on, boats against the current, born back ceaselessly," indicates that it is impossible for those who give in to desire to fulfill their dream.

The theme of idolatry is further emphasized in the scene in which Nick stares for half an hour at Gatsby's mansion in much the same way as Kant stares at the church steeples.[74] Nick is no philosopher, but there is a certain existential curiosity in his attempt to discover some kind of meaning in the increasingly dramatic events of that summer. However, this meaning is so limited that it can be summed up in Gatsby's incredible ability to hope, against all odds.

In *The Great Gatsby*, God has absconded, just like the Gnostic God of the Spirit. Wilson is the only person in the novel who calls on God, but his God is strange and estranged. Wilson does not belong to any church or know any church.[75] His is a new god, symbolically linked to a billboard. Wilson is transfixed by the material god, the god who sees everything and cannot be fooled but does not care, like the eyes of Doctor T. J. Eckleburg. He is depicted as lifeless and grey, as someone who has been killed by desire before he kills himself. In the enormous advertisement of Doctor

T. J. Eckleburg, a change in religious outlook is evident. The Christian God has been replaced by a new and inactive god, who sees everything. This god, devoid of desire and compassion, broods over the godless valley of ashes with his blue eyes, his yellow glasses and nonexistent nose, illustrating the nothingness that concludes the novel.

5

Desire in *Death of a Salesman*

Therefore,

Their sons grow suicidally beautiful

At the beginning of October,

And gallop terribly against each other's bodies.

> —James Wright, "Autumn Begins
> in Martins Ferry, Ohio"

In the book *The American Dream: A Short History of an Idea That Shaped a Nation*, Jim Cullen focuses on what he considers the six main themes that characterize the American dream: religious freedom, the quest for equality, the Declaration of Independence, upward mobility, home ownership, and fame and fortune.[1] Arthur Miller's *Death of a Salesman* depicts a distorted version of this dream. The first three of Cullen's themes do not play a central role in *Death of a Salesman*. However, the last three, upward mobility, home ownership, and especially fame and fortune, are core "values" for the Lomans, the family at the center of Miller's drama. In the light of the dream, we understand why the house and car are so important in the play. Even more significant, though, the central character Willy Loman's approach to life verges on a decayed version of the American dream, in which talent and hard work are subordinated to fame. This modern delusion, in which a charismatic personality is a necessity, in which physical beauty is almost valued more highly than wealth, and in which the elect are those who do not have to try too hard,[2] contains the elements of Willy's American dream.

Willy Loman has no past, no tradition to cling to. He is a prisoner of the here and now. The cheapness of his existence is highlighted by a lack of tradition and history. To cope with this void, he only allows himself to see the world through the rose-tinted ideals and slightly brutal work ethics of a salesman. In the course of the play, the meaninglessness of the life of a salesman, once something outwardly able to fill his life with meaning, is gradually revealed.

In the play, Willy confesses to an imaginary Ben that he feels kind of temporary about himself.[3] As a child, he was abandoned by his father. Lacking a father figure, he turned to his older brother, Ben, who did not really care about his younger brother, only his own career and success, a success partly based on cheating others. Like Jay Gatsby, Ben has taken shortcuts on the road to success and wealth. Thus, Willy's basic male models from early childhood on were his father, who abandoned him, and Ben, who was driven by a brutal desire for success. Willy is totally spellbound by Ben and his success and, therefore, totally spellbound by the American dream—without ever considering the premises or the futility of the dream.

Willy's background hints not so much at why he does not succeed in business, as at why he deceives himself and his family. His past has made him vulnerable to the outward trappings of the American dream. Not once do we hear Willy Loman reflect on the reality of the dream, on the fact that there will be very few winners and very many losers. According to Brian Parker, Willy and his family are victims of the deterioration of this dream. Parker sees Willy's philosophy as a reflection of the personality cult of Dale Carnegie in which one wins friends and influences others for the purpose of gain.[4]

Willy thinks of himself in terms of what he does; his identity lies in his work title. He is not interested in who he really is or his inner value. His life philosophy focuses on success, primarily in sports and business. He has no other ideals, no religion or philosophy, to balance such an ideal. Willy thinks that if he is not successful, he cannot deserve to be loved by his family.[5] All his life, he has compensated for his unhappy childhood by clinging to the belief that being well liked is all that is necessary. Willy believes in the cult of personality and in the importance of charm. His dream of being successful in business and sport, as in other areas of life, is clearly based on the romantic and virility-based notion that one can make one's mark by outdoing others. Willy believes in the romantic personality, the person who is gifted by nature, who is looked up to and admired by others, and who does not have to work hard to attain success.

In Willy's view, natural strength and natural charm are enough, and he believes that these qualities are exactly what

Biff has. Willy sees in Biff a kind of internalized superiority, evident in such statements as: "You got greatness in you."[6] He just cannot understand that his son is lost "in the greatest country in the world" since he is a young man with such "personal attractiveness."[7]

Looks are clearly important. Biff is described as a young Hercules,[8] while both Biff and Happy are called Adonises. In his father's eyes, Biff stands above the normal moral limitations because of his looks and talent in sports; the fact that he breaks the rules simply highlights his superiority. Thus, Willy laughs proudly when Biff is accused of theft and claims that if anyone else had stolen something, there would have been an uproar.[9] While the young Biff, like Hercules with a golden helmet, is glorified by his father as a young god, "And the sun, the sun all around him,"[10] he later returns to his parent's home as a thirty-four-year-old misfit. The strong, ruthless high-school graduate, with the looks of Adonis, has striven in accordance with his father and Uncle Ben's law of the jungle but has not been able to hold down a job.

Willy has taught his sons the shortcut to success: success begins by being well liked. If you are well liked, you are not even obliged to abide by the law. Therefore, Willy accepts that the young Biff steals timber and basketballs, not understanding that this ethical laissez-faire attitude could later cultivate arrogance, laziness, and ruthlessness. Justified by his brother Ben's law of the jungle, Willy accepts that there will be a certain dishonesty among the elect, the likeable, as an indication of superiority. According to Matthew C. Roudané, stealing in the play illustrates a stealing of identity, a loss of self.[11]

Willy, although hard working himself, does not convey to his sons that hard work is the real way to success. Blinded by his narcissism, he cannot see that education, which he lacks, could contribute to his sons' success. Moreover, by emphasizing personality and sport to such a degree, Willy actually limits his sons' chances for success.

The American Dream

The more Willy tries to enhance his sons' success, the more they are channeled into failure. Willy's American dream consists only of success, not of the hard work that is a prerequisite for success. Willy has become like Ben, inclined to take shortcuts in order to attain his goal; but, unlike his brother, his desire for success ends in failure. This causes readers to question the dream itself. According to Cullen, the real problem with the American dream is that it is too incomplete a vessel to contain the longings that elude human expression or comprehension: "We never reach the Coast we think we see."[12] Thus, it is something related to the desires behind the dream that causes the dream to turn sour. If we examine the models who have represented this mighty dream, Willy seems to have been influenced by the ideals of such men as Andrew Jackson, America's president from 1829 to 1837, who was born poor, lived in near wilderness, and became successful due to his own strength and iron will. From this perspective, Ben becomes, in Willy's eyes, the ultimate living model for his sons to imitate.

However, there is one essential ingredient lacking in Willy's American dream: He does not really believe in self-improvement, but rather in natural charisma. In this respect Willy, like Jefferson for example, thinks that there is

The conflict between Willy and Biff is clearly destined to end in tragedy. "Double mediation," Girard's term for reciprocal imitation, between father and son arises because each of them desires success through the other. But in both cases, the desire for success turns into degrading failure, and they begin to blame each other. Willy shifts continuously between praising and despising Biff. He can only accept the successful side of his son, a side that is constantly waning. Because Biff is a part of himself, he cannot accept anything but success. However, the pressure being put on Biff causes him to fail repeatedly. In one sense, his failure, like his father's, comes down to a deep desire to subvert the other's desire. Biff cannot succeed since that would mean that he has, existentially, become a fake like his father. Willy and Biff have become each other's stumbling blocks. Biff, however, has partially perceived this illusion, but instead of feeling sorry for his father, he considers him pathetic.

The previous time Biff had come home, Willy had thrown him out because Biff called him a fake.[14] Biff swears to his mother that this time he will behave,[15] but when Willy enters the room, they immediately begin blaming each other. The worldly success. This has created a configuration in which the mother, Linda, always takes the side of the father. She does not know about her husband's infidelity, so she does not know that Biff is unconsciously defending her and punishing Willy for having betrayed her.

Biff not only witnesses Willy in bed with a young lady, he also discovers that Willy has given his lover stockings belonging to Biff's own mother,[17] a very scarce and luxurious item after World War II. Thus, stockings become a symbol of Willy's betrayal, and in the play Willy cannot stand the sight of his wife mending her stockings.

The rivalry is enhanced by Willy's feeling of guilt toward Biff. Every time Willy looks at Biff, he is reminded of his infidelity and immediately feels exposed. After Biff witnesses Willy's affair in a hotel room in Baltimore, their relationship is irretrievably ruined. Both men live with this secret. Willy is terrified that Biff will expose him and, at the same time, is guilt ridden. Every time Willy encounters Biff, he feels guilty, and this make him behave irrationally.

The hotel incident is often considered to be the key to the Loman family's dysfunctional behavior. The scenes before the hotel-room scene build up neatly toward an unavoidable rivalry between father and son. Willy has, up to this incident, been the young Biff's main role model, and the boy believes blindly in his father's ideals, ideals that in substance may—if there is no outer goal, no enemy to conquer, and no jungle to escape—create extreme rivalry within one's family. Rivalry between father and son, however, is usually more complex than, for example, rivalry between friends and colleagues because it usually supplants by metamorphosis a deep love; thus, love and loyalty are transformed into spite due to an identification crisis, and friendship is transformed into enemy twinship.

This distortion of the truth results in Linda blaming Biff for Willy's attempted suicide. At this point, the play develops from a tale of domestic conflicts to a tragedy. As in the case of Oedipus Rex, this happens because vital information is withheld. Oedipus has no knowledge of who his real parents are, while Linda has no knowledge of having been deceived.

Although the father–son relationship is complex, the system of desire is basically the same as in other relations. From such a perspective, the Oedipus complex is not an adequate model because it is a preconstructed model, while desire is governed by no other model than the other's desire. According to Girard, all desires are mimetic and based on the other's desire. It is therefore essential that the father is capable of eliminating potential rivalry before it becomes real and endangers family relations. Biff has lost faith in his prime imitative model and does not seem able to find an alternative. On the one hand, he hates his father and, on the other hand, he embraces his father's ideals of success, and this creates a double bind that leads to failure. Every time Biff attempts to succeed in business, he is reminded of his father's betrayal, and he subconsciously sets himself up to fail.

Seen through the lenses of imitative desire, the play becomes a drama about liberation from the other. However, the play's fundamental insight, its genius, is its description of how desire works. Miller describes desire in such a way that it is only concerned with the unfulfilled. Desire has turned Willy and Biff into a state where everyday reality means less and less. They are possessed by each other. Even when Biff is not at home, Willy is still preoccupied with the conflict with his son, and the tragedy lies in the fact that Willy will not alter his belief in personality and success. As spectators, the audience follows Willy through the last twenty-four hours of his life in which the world is gradually closing in on him.

Salvation in Nature

Death of a Salesman is based on a dark world-view. There seems to be no escape and no reconciliation possible within the frame of the characters' lives. Rivalry and conflict color the characters' outlook on life. While there is always a glimpse of freedom lurking around the corner, this is always destroyed by desire. The vitality of outdoor life is clearly an ideal for the characters. This is evident in Biff's claim that his family should be working on the land, out in the open air. Similarly, Willy admires the countryside from the road and feels claustrophobic in the mechanized urban environment.[18] He talks longingly of nature, the country, and the open air. Biff is even more frank about his yearning for a healthy life in the country: "We should be mixing cement on some open plain—or carpenters. A carpenter is allowed family, Miller is touching upon the barrenness of modern life. Like T. S. Eliot's poem *The Waste Land*,[21] *Death of a Salesman* depicts contemporary Western urban culture as sterile and lifeless, a place where people are obsessed with novelty. However, in Eliot's poem, contemporary trends and materialism are echoed by a richer and more fertile past; beneath the cultural barrenness lie seeds of moral regeneration. This regeneration is indicated in *Death of a Salesman*, in act 2, when Willy wants to go out and buy some seeds and see things growing again. But according to Linda "nothing'll grow any more."[22] As in *The Waste Land*, growth is associated with cruelty. For example, April, the month of fertility, is the cruelest of all months, "breeding / Lilacs out of dead land."[23] In *Death of a Salesman*, Willy experiences a similar barrenness, the same cruelty, claiming that "there is not a breath of fresh air in the neighborhood. The grass don't grow any more, you can't raise a carrot in the backyard."[24] The earth, in *Death of a Salesman*, refers more concretely to the earth as such, but in both the poem and the play, barrenness seems to be the result of desire. According to Eliot, one finds, under the dry earth, traits of violence, hidden by hysterical and empty expressions of contemporary culture. Beneath the contemporary shallowness, the poem alludes to sacrifice; dead corpses and dry bones that dogs threaten to dig up again.[25] In both the play and the poem, the decline of earth and culture are viewed as a unit, mixed up with death.

Infidelity and Barrenness

The barrenness of existence gradually reveals itself, not as a lack of contact with nature, but as cruelty in human relations. In both *The Waste Land* and *Death of a Salesman* infidelity seems to be a source of cultural emptiness. The low life of a salesman, which is the basic setting in Miller's play, is also evident in Eliot's poem. Mr. Eugenides, the Smyrna merchant, becomes a symbol of the cultural decay.[26] Like Willy Loman, Mr. Eugenides is loud, vulgar, and contemporary. The currants in his pocket are a symbol of his utilitarian world-view based on physical nutrition. The decay of manners and morals are further emphasized by the small house agent clerk with staring eyes: "One of the low on whom assurance sits / As a silk hat on a Bradford millionaire."[27] The house agent, a salesman like Willy, is vulgar, and his attempt to seduce is devoid of tenderness. His only purpose is physical self-satisfaction. The somber modernism as shown in these works reveals, at its heart, a broken trust between man and woman.

While Willy clings to his shallow ideals of being well liked and successful, and teaches his son to cash in on his personal attractiveness, the characters in *The Waste Land* delve into vulgarity, the "Jug Jug to dirty ears,"[28] where tradition is lost and replaced by horoscopes and loveless sexuality, causing indifference and a lack of communication.

Sources to Regeneration

In Eliot's wasteland experience there is reconciliation, some sort of hope of continuation through the renewal of genuine European cultural values. The intertextuality of the poem creates a dialectic between a rich past and a barren contemporary world. The hopelessness of the here and now, however, is not absolute. It is debased but has, nevertheless, evolved from a rich and fertile past. *The Waste Land* ends with images from an ancient religious and literary tradition that promotes fertility and peace, indicating a future of regeneration and reconciliation.

In contrast, the characters in *Death of a Salesman* are lacking in a cultural heritage, myths, or religion. The Loman family is lost in their distorted American dream, with no reinvigorating ideas or ideals to help them find a better existence. The desire to move out into the countryside is clearly an ideal but can never materialize because of the rivalry between father and son. The freedom to break out, start anew, and do something they really enjoy can only be realized if the characters give up their current existence in which the real objects of desire constantly vanish due to the fierce father–son rivalry. This rivalry has become so complex that Willy would actually never be able to be reconciled with it. In their enclosed suburban Brooklyn environment, there is no reinvigorating past and no invigorating future. Their world is a closed world because they have, in their own eyes and those of others, become losers in their competition to succeed.

After the disastrous dinner at the restaurant, Willy tries one last time to get hold of some seeds to plant.[29] The desire to see something grow comes after the father and son have revealed their personal drought: Willy has been fired, and Biff has run out of a job interview after stealing a fountain pen. The seeds represent Willy's last hope. They seem to be the nearest the play gets to any symbol of renewal. Thus, the seeds represent hope for growth and renewal after every other hope is gone. Nature represents a stubborn drive for renewal, but is nevertheless unable to save the characters from their hellish existence. The seeds could, in a different context, be seen to represent real renewal, like the regenerating water-symbols at the end of *The Waste Land*. However, it would be misleading to see any real reconciliation in *Death of a Salesman*, either between Biff and Willy or in nature. The only catharsis is when Biff begins to cry and Willy, for a brief moment, understands that his son actually loves him.

6

Desire in Lana Del Rey

No matter where!
No matter where!
As Long as it is out of this world
—Baudelaire

Elizabeth Grant, better known under the name Lana Del Rey, is a singer and songwriter who subjectively goes in depth to discover the foundation of the culture she lives within. In her world, which comprises a never-ending yearning for oneness with a beloved, a pantheon of enticing cultural icons arises, magnified in her perspective, trustworthy and enchanting objects of her desire. Lana seems to have such a total, non-moralistic, and in many ways uncompromising focus on desire that it becomes a valuable source for understanding how desire changes and develops in relationships. Thus, her songs and her world view become poignant contemporary expressions of desire, and they help us to understand the way desire is experienced in our contemporary Western world.

Lana Del Rey's preoccupation with the other, the beloved, is in all its different manifestations built on a desire for the other, a strong urge to be acknowledged, accepted, and loved. Even when the relationship with the other is degrading and the feedback from the beloved is cold and brutal, indomitable desire, fueled by the beloved's iconic appearance, seems to be based on an enduring belief that there will one day be a fundamental breakthrough. This repetitiveness reveals, in my view, the core content of the nature of desire, a force that promises so much but, in reality, gives back so little.

The American Dream

In Lana's textual world,[1] the American dream simply exists. Therefore, it does not represent something one strives for. In a way, she has already achieved the dream—in her way.

> *Everything I want I have*
> *Money, notoriety and rivieras.*
> ("Without You")

Thus, the most interesting aspects about it are neither fame nor success, but instead the darker notions of the dream, the destructive desires that the dream entails. Lana does not really believe in self-improvement, a typical trait of the American dream, but instead strongly believes in following her heart's desire. One might say that her dreams are distorted versions of the American dream, as these dreams eventually end in rivalry, coldness, and ethical laissez-faire, thus paving the way for tragedy.

In *The American Dream: A Short History of an Idea That Shaped a Nation*, Jim Cullen mentions religious freedom, quest for equality, the Declaration of Independence, upward mobility, home ownership, and fame and fortune as important ingredients in the American dream.[2] Five of them do not play a central role in Del Rey's songs. However, fame and fortune, especially if fortune means success, is an aspect that Lana often comments on, although she makes it clear that she does not really believe in it because it fails to yield any real satisfaction in love relations. Thus, Lana's dreams are those of an updated, modern conception of the American dream, in which a charismatic personality is a crucial necessity, in which physical beauty is valued more highly than wealth and in which the elect are those who follow their own heart and who in reality do not have to try too hard—in the traditional sense. It must be noted that at a certain stage, when following one's heart's desire, the dream shares many of the attributes of narcissism. Thus, in Lana's songs, as in Arthur Miller's *Death of a Salesman*, certain desires inherent in the American dream are the very things that turn it sour.

In Lana Del Rey's world, it is the man who is always acting as if he is self-sufficient. Initially he is the cool guy, and frequently an incarnation of the American dream, reminding the listener of some version of a well-established and desirable icon. The icon seems to transform desire in order to become reality per se, motivated by a possessive urge toward self-fulfillment. Gradually, by its imitative nature, the repetitive element changes the scene so that the attraction becomes more and more possessive. The repetitive aspect of desire in Lana's songs is exceptionally strong, as desire today, compared with the past, renews us continuously through fashion, films, advertisement, etc., and, in this respect, continually renews our hope that this time around, we will achieve what we long for.

Desire for God

In the same way as Lana gives a twist to the concept of the American dream, she also alters our understanding of religion insofar as it primarily relates to love between lovers. In the song "Religion," the lovers' unity seems complete. It is so perfect that it becomes somehow otherworldly. In Del Rey's songs, it is normally all about the I's longing; here, however, the beloved is himself genuinely seeking love and love alone. The religious dimension, as well as the anthropological and erotic, is based upon a perfect union in which her life is formed in harmony with his. In this respect, we see that Lana's religion, despite its Gnostic and idealistic tendencies, seems based on both sexual satisfaction and unity with the beloved. In so many of her songs, sexuality is initially a great liberating force, until it becomes a "skandalon," a triggered snare that degrades one's personality.

Lana describes a process whereby one is blind to mimetic rivalry, and instead sees in the love for the other a desire that will last forever. However, this idolization is also an idolization of the self. The more the self is worshiped, the more one's worshiped models become rivals to the self that now loves its self more, and in the words of Girard, create "a cult that turns to hatred."[3]

In "Gods & Monsters" Lana sees herself as an angel in a garden of evil. The atmosphere, already from line one, is more desperate than in most of her songs. The crude and unpleasant ambiance sets it apart from her typical setting. In this fallen, frightening state, there is no option other than "doing anything that I needed". In such a hostile atmosphere, no medicine except fame, dope, and love is able to help her get by. In "Gods & Monsters" there is a pronounced hostility toward religion, and the I chooses to live as if God is dead, preferring a life in accordance with the 1960s' bohemian lifestyle of Jim Morrison. The natural, if restrained, relationship with God, as in some of Del Rey's other songs, is no longer evident. The world seems so tainted by sexual cynicism that to survive one must lose one's innocence. The strained atmosphere is caused by life imitating art. The unnatural world, a far cry from Walt Whitman's imitation of the natural and healthy, is a world turned upside down. The I, deeply emotionally disturbed, therefore tries to escape from the natural world by imitating art. The imitation of art in real life also seems to be the source behind the veneration of cultural icons such as Elvis and Marilyn Monroe, both the victims of fame and prisoners of a sterile and unnatural existence.

The "fiery beacon" metaphor marvelously illustrates the concept of desire, of shining a beam of light on everyone, without any inherent virtue oneself. This lack of identity, this feeling of being no one and, at the same time, everyone, is elegantly fused together into an existence where God is dead. As in Baudelaire's poem, "Anywhere Out of the World," the

I, after pondering on the human possibilities, cries out in his longing for something totally otherworldly:

No matter where!
No matter where!
As long as it's out of the world!

In Lana's songs, God is usually obvious but not a power toward which one turns to experience love. The I sees no necessary distinction between Eros and agape. Nor is there any qualitative distinction between the two, and there is no reflection on the nature of God's love. God is just there. Considering her theological education at Fordham University with its Jesuit influences,[4] Lana's religious views, interpreted from her lyrics, seem surprisingly neutral or a-religious in the sense that God, and the whole concept of Christian love, is seldom seen as a contrast to, and never really an alternative to, the love of the lovers. This, of course, must be viewed in the light of today's pop and rock music, where the slightest hint of a positive relationship with church dogma would likely ruin sales and preclude fame. God in Lana's world is

and Jesus (best friend) changes to Whitman and Monaco and diamonds. Religious and cultural icons fuse. The Virgin Mary prays in two instances for I's broken mind. However, the third time, everything is ignited by desire. Mary is no longer praying; she is swaying softly to her heart's desire.

The dualism between the sacred and the profane is an issue, but does not really matter in content, as it all amounts to an all-encompassing desire toward the lover, the you. There is hardly any distinction between the religious and the mundane. Like in the song "Religion," the search is not about God but about finding unity with the beloved. The transcendence Lana yearns for is not brought about by a transcendental God of love. It is not exactly a substitute for it either. However, the religious entails an inherent transcendence, brought about by a desire for someone. The main religious trait in her songs is of an anthropological nature, out of which men become gods or at least take on some kind of transcendental quality. Viewed against the background of religious beliefs, her otherworldliness seems related to Gnosticism, where the world is evil and chaotic. The sensual, however, represents the opposite to Lana than it did to Origen, a thinker with Gnostic tendencies, where sexuality is seen as the primal sin. Her view of this world as basically cruel shapes her Gnosticism based on the concept that one does not have to live a moral life to be saved and thus can "intemperately serve the lusts of the flesh and say that one renders flesh to the flesh and spirit to the spirit."[5] However, the hopelessness and helplessness when encountering the disappointments of her Gnosticism seem to stem from her Catholicism.

Girard and the "Skandalon" Caused by Desire

Reality changes by imitative desire, debasing the inner person and causing a breakdown of values. Drugs, fame, a desire to get fucked hard may all be seen as substitutions for genuine love. The effect of trying to please one's beloved becomes a "skandalon," a term that Girard uses to express the ultimate negative effect caused by a relational process where the goal of one's desire is gradually lost, and in the end, by the working of desire, only obstacles are left.[6] Thus, the "skandalon" is the stumbling block, and at its most extreme can lead to murder and madness. The "skandalon" is a temptation-causing attraction to the extent that it becomes an obstacle. "Skandalon" means forming an obstacle that attracts victims and becomes an irresistible temptation.[7]

The "skandalon" involves an obsessional obstacle, raised by imitation, and is the darker effect of mimetic desire, with all its empty ambitions and ridiculous antagonisms. It is the model exerting its special form of temptation. The "skandalon" is the obstacle/model created by mimetic desire that gradually becomes an inexhaustible source of morbid fascination.[8] "Skandalon" is the trap, luring one into degrading human relations. The person possessed by the other dreams of a life blossoming in fulfillment. It seems only a question of time before initiation and fulfillment are reached. While giving the false impression that suffering is only a prelude to some kind of divine initiation—and that love will at last break through—its realization finally becomes the sunset of desire.

"Skandalon" in Lana's Universe

Lana's universe must be seen in the context of a world with fewer and fewer barriers providing people with more and more opportunities to become fascinating obstacles for one another, and therefore to become the cause of reciprocal scandal. The scandalous would not be scandalous if it did not form an irresistible and impossible example offering itself for imitation as both model and antimodel at the same time.[9] This double bind between model and antimodel is the buildup to the sacred setting in so many of Lana Del Rey's songs. The more desire mounts in Lana's love for the other, the more strongly she experiences the other's resistance.

The mythmaking in Lana's world consists in the I not being able to see through the snares of the cool behavior of the other. Thus, the obstacle is turned into a catalyst for her desires, although this creates a distorted and uneven relationship. It is this repetitive movement, the desire to be loved together with the experience of coldness, that defines Lana's experience of love. In some instances, often where the text is more an entity (but the content weaker), she seems to fake a union at the expense of truth as existential darkness. The depressiveness stemming from metaphysical desire comes from the fact that one constantly knocks on the doors that are firmly closed and searches only where nothing is to be found.[10]

Master and Slave

In "Ultraviolence" Lana mixes violence and love in such a way that in some instances those phenomena become totally entangled. The entanglement seems to hollow out the soul or the inner being, making one feel submissive and wanting to make the other the master. This want is not a genuine want, more a fast fix out of an awkward relationship. However, the violence committed by the beloved against her tells her that this kind of love is limited.

The fact that the beloved hits her brings forth nostalgia from childhood, like fights between siblings, but seems somewhat queer in relation to a grown man who, despite having an adolescent mind, is otherwise cool and self-confident.

At the same time, as so often in Lana's songs (and in real life), the feeling of love sustains despite outrageous behavior.

Hegel's Master and Slave

Hegel usually limits conflictual relationships to a desire between a master and a slave. There is no third party, no mediator manipulating the desires involved. Nor is there any attempt in Hegel's work to depict the structure of erotic desire. The structure is built on a desire for *acknowledgment*. Thus, desire in Hegel's *Phenomenology of the Spirit* is explained as desire for acknowledgment. In Lana's universe the I starts by being the slave, while the beloved is the master. Lana's notion of desire resembles this understanding of master and slave in many respects. Objects govern desire for Hegel, and the main object is the other. According to Hegel, the other is a prolongation of self-desire. However, in the same manner as Lana, he places little emphasis on the objectivity and concreteness surrounding the interpersonal relationships between the master and slave.

Both Lana's and Hegel's concepts of desire are initially *self-consciousness*. Hegel defines self-consciousness as desire.[11] The human's initial stage of being is a desiring self-consciousness. In this initial phase of existence, desire is directed against the self. Self-consciousness is, as Allen Wood claims, a desire, a striving of the ego against otherness.[12] The self-consciousness in Hegel, which has an instinctive need to preserve its autonomy, is in Lana's world more or less completely loosened from any biological or cultural foundation.

In "Shades of Cool" the I is in rivalry in order to be with this unattainable male who lives his life in shades of cool. This "guy," however, is unchangeable, unable to receive anybody's love. This apparent unchangeability becomes the attraction. The I's delusion is her belief in this state of coolness. If she had perceived the guy's inability to love and change, the spell would be broken—which it partly does in the song "High by the Beach." However, by trying to keep the rival, her boyfriend, at arm's length, the possessiveness continues. Just as in Girard's triangular concept of desire, there is gradually no longer any real object, only the desire to outdo the rival.[13]

The I mistakes the guy's coolness as a great hindrance for her love, whereas it is actually desire itself that is the main obstacle. Half seeing that this relationship is unreal, the I, in her tender hopes, upholds the dream of being the preferred girl.

According to Hegel, the desires arising from self-consciousness will provoke antagonistic desires when confronted by the other's desire. The satisfaction of desire is only preliminary and brings no real satisfaction, because it creates no freedom in relation to the object. On the contrary, new objects are continually required for its satisfaction.[14] This explains the ongoing zest for fulfillment in Lana's songs. However, self-consciousness can only acquire freedom by means of another self-consciousness.[15] The fluid self-consciousness is an imitation of the other; the doubling of desire, the "I" that is "we."[16] While Hegel lays emphasis on the acknowledgment of the other, the process of recognition or harmonization, where the master acknowledges the slave, seems, in Lana's love relationships, to take the opposite course. Here desire is so strong in its initial stages that it eventually hinders any happy union. Lana's expressions of desire in relationships in this respect are similar to Girard's mimetic theory, as there is an asymmetrical development, where the lovers are hindered by each other's negative identification. Hegel places little emphasis on asymmetrical development (where desire to profess uniqueness creates similarities)—even when the master's acceptance represents a change from violence to concern.

Hegel propagates a dialectical development where desire basically is a *subject–subject relationship*. This subject–subject relationship has a double structure. It means that the other—understood as a part of a linear structure—can change desires. Change therefore requires togetherness.

Thus the movement is simply the double movement of the two self-consciousnesses. Each sees the other do the same as it does; each does itself what it demands of the other, and therefore also does what it does only in so far as the other does the same. Action by one side only would be useless because what is to happen can only be brought about by both.[17]

In Lana's songs, the beloved never changes; that is the price he pays for playing the cool guy. However, playing the cool guy means that the development in their affair is a development where everything worsens. The coolness, which Lana seldom tries to unmask in its entirety, reveals the other's weaknesses but, at the same time, also exposes her own dream illusions.

Hegel interprets desire as a means to achieving a goal. The struggle between life and death, where there is a striving toward the other's death,[18] is paradoxically the way in which the master and the slave ultimately acknowledge each other. Hegel's acknowledgment, when stripped of its abstract language, demonstrates a clear affinity with the Christian concept of loving one's neighbor. This kind of altruism is absent in Lana's world, as the I's only focus from the beginning is a fascination either with the beloved or with some cultural icon. However, despite Hegel's Christian conclusion, positing the goal as the Spirit's total knowledge revealed as a dream of absolute (in)sight is something that Lana strives for in all her subjectivity.[19]

In the preliminary stages of the relationship between

master and slave, the master's independence is based on his control over things. In the song "Cruel World" Lana paints a picture of an innocent girl among violent men. However, the surroundings are blurry, and the scene might just as well be taking place in an upper-class environment as in outdoor surroundings or in some kind of run-down place. In "Cruel World" everybody seems to be relieved when the man, a drinker, a drug addict, a partygoer, is gone. The zest for freedom takes a frenetic path, and she seems to find solace by taking control over the man's gun and Bible, likely symbols of the tools he uses to exercise power.

Neither Hegel nor Lana see the injustice or (feigned) superiority as desire according to the master's desire. The vulnerable state of mind is rather a desire to feel accepted by the master. The master's need for acceptance by the slave, however, is never a vital part of the affairs Lana describes. Neither are her desires directly based on a desire for the master's things (possessions). "The lord puts himself into relation with both of these moments, to a thing as such, the object of desire, and to the consciousness for which thinghood is the essential characteristic."[20]

Both in Lana's and Hegel's world there is a desire for acknowledgment, and it is the acknowledgment that is the path to freedom.[21] Thinghood, as it is both an object and a consciousness, is thus secondary, both in Hegel's and Lana's concept of desire. Both locate desire in relation to the other in metaphysical and nonbiological categories—despite Lana's sexually explicit lyrics and Hegel's understanding of self-desire founded on biology. In Hegel's case, self-desire is directly related to maintaining and reproducing life.

Violence

In the song "Bel Air," the urge to see one's love borders on madness, or at least on a lack of self-control. The beautiful surroundings described in "Bel Air" indicate great wealth but reveal an emptiness caused by unfulfilled longings. Out of this longing emerges an appeal not to feel afraid or ashamed. The desired person's reluctance does not seem to have any effect on the I. He is divine, and his love will help lead the way to war. Violence, war, and love seem to be entangled in Lana's world, ending up in some sort of existential masochism. This theme becomes clearer by its polarity in "Honeymoon," where the man with a record of violence is so elusive that one wants to either fight or marry him.

Desire always seems to have the upper hand in the way the beginnings never meet the end. Relationships end, either in pure longing or in some kind of degradation. Desire changes the course, and the economy of love, illustrated in "Million Dollar Man," stands in direct disproportion to his outer appearance of possessing wealth and coolness.

Triangular Desire and Violence

In "Cola (Pussy)" there is a triangular scene where the lovers yearn to escape. The I claims that her lover's wife probably will not mind. The perspective is somewhat distorted, perhaps seen through the influence of drugs. Juxtapositions of metaphors create alternative allegiances. The I falls asleep, wrapped in an American flag, and she wears her diamonds in an area of Los Angeles where the sick and homeless live.

It may appear that this homelessness is spiritual due to its nonmaterialism, but it could just as well be the effects of mimetic desire in the extreme, where only the obstacles count. The scene seems to suggest a condition in which all objects have disappeared. The only one left is the desired other who opens up and lets her in, although only partially. There is something disturbing, a perverted kind of puritanism created by an excess of desire, and the I feels no obligation to any others than these who are able to evoke desire. From this desire comes veneration for cultural icons, the pantheon of Hollywood gods enabling us to assume fake identities.

Postsacrificial societies permit a greater degree of competition, which leads to more advanced technological stages and in turn creates more potential destructiveness. Nonsacrificial desire seldom legitimizes violence, while, at the same time, it can turn out to be potentially extremely violent. The violent consequence of modern desire can be linked partly to Paul Virilio's theory of *dromology*,[22] where speed is seen as violence, and where secular violence operates with enormous speed, thus distancing and modifying the guilt of the violator. This violence comes as subdued versions in Lana's songs. However, desire is seen in relation to driving fast and losing oneself in speed. Speed is a liberator, as well as something aesthetic and beautiful. The process of accelerating, speeding, living fast and dangerous indicates potential violence. In this respect, speed can be seen as affiliated with desire. Speed seems to be a direct consequence of desire. In "Diet Mountain Dew," cars and roller coasters enhance lust and frustration, as if to overcome an unbearable relationship and create some kind of unity.

Love

In a DVD on Lana Del Rey's life called *The Greatest Story Never Told*, Lana says in one interview, when asked about love, that her main themes concerning love are to "honor it while lost, staying strong in the midst of true love lost, and staying hopeful and soft when things get difficult, as they do, for everyone."[23] Love in Lana's world is strictly limited to love between lovers. It is often one-sided and always based on attraction. Love, or more precisely the wish to love, has somewhat taken the place of religion. Eros has replaced agape. In "Swan Song," one is presented with the romantic idea of giving up work in order to follow one's free desire. This song, perhaps because it exudes no tension, seems textually weaker than most of her songs. The song is built on dreams of something perfect and otherworldly, an aesthetic dream that if we see it in context of Lana's life philosophy as a whole, will never be realized.

In "24" we once again find ourselves in a scene where the I admires the rough gangster type. However, the insights given from the relationship make her act with greater caution. Admiration is not blind and total. She sees danger in bad company, emphasized in a metaphor of contagion: getting fleas. The gangster, who spends half of the day in bed with her, thinks only of violence and carnage. She sees that he pays a high price for his violent ways by being so "cold to touch and hard to reach." The mild melody seems out of tune with the text. Its distorted effect reminds one of a David Lynch movie. Also in "Art Deco" Lana depicts the dichotomy between a lack of confidence and the unstoppable desire for something more. She tries to ignore the other, the obstacle, in order to reach this "more." This causes an irresolvable double bind where the last sentence, "We were born to be free," is the absolute antithesis of the nervous tension in the whole party atmosphere. It can be read as a comment on the club queen's lack of freedom, causing an urge to get away from everything.

De Rougemont's Theory of Love

In Denis de Rougemont's book *Love in the Western World*, which deals with the nature of love and its decline in the West, love expresses a love for love, not a love for the other person involved in lovemaking. It is a narcissistic love where the lover's self-magnification is emphasized more than the relationship with the beloved.[24] Love is ignited through obstacles, even for obstacles. If there were no obstacles, there would be no love. So, in reality there is no love, only love for obstacles. According to de Rougemont, within this masochistic realm of love for obstacles there is a pathological fear of falling in love in a simple, straightforward manner.[25]

Lana's experience of love as a temptation to continually fall in love seems tinged with an awe for cultural icons that express many of the same romantic ideas as de Rougemont describes. However, she is never afraid of falling in love. Most of her songs are about recklessly falling in love and thinking that it will last forever.

The myth, which de Rougemont calls the *passion-myth*, magnifies and divinizes unhappy, nonsensual love and is actually a love for nothingness, for death.[26] This unhappy love takes a slightly different turn in "Freak." However, all the ingredients for romantic love are present in this song. The focus is solely on the one favored person. The notion is that one needs nothing other than being loved by this one person. This romanticism is upheld by the coldness of the beloved. It reminds one of Petrarch's sonnet 188 where love only thrives when the lovers are apart: "If when afar to burn, to freeze when near."

De Rougemont considers the development of the passion-myth as the source of decay in the realm of love. Its literature weaves the lies, which enhance the desires for loveless love. Lana puts all her hope in the one who is distinguished from the rest. Her lovers are all romantic heroes, if not in the classical manner, then at least in a Hollywood manner. Moreover, the romances never wind up lasting very long.

De Rougemont claims that the passion-myth generates violence.[27] In a world where love has been perverted into self-love and a desire for obstacles, there are no limits to such activities, created in order to avoid real love. Nationalism, according to de Rougemont, is caught up in the same desires, where private passions are projected into a sterile and loveless concept of a nation.[28] In "American," Lana describes a man that she dearly loves, a prototype of an American hero and at the same time a sexually desirable object: tall, tanned, and able to make girls go wild. However, the song touches on sickness, indicating a kind of national trauma. As in "National Anthem," it is the darkness of the American dream Lana wants to explore. There is a sort of uncertain irony in both these songs, as if she ponders: Shall I be ironic? "National Anthem" ends in the typical Lana manner, by claiming an everlasting love for the beloved, who has become estranged, in order to uphold his image as wildly attractive. In this way, against the backdrop of

Naturalistic Sensuality

De Rougemont claims that naturalistic sensuality is actually the same as Romance-desires, only sublimated to fit into a more animalistic ideal.[32] In the context of de Rougemont's antinaturalism, Lana's Romanticism is more sexually explicit. The I, however, is seldom playing the role of a seducer. The sympathy one feels toward the I comes from the desperation of her never-ending belief in the beloved. There is no critique other than desperation. In "Fucked My Way Up to the Top," she describes both lovers as losers. However, the I, at least, has passed the test. Her partner, however, by being a loser, makes her love him, and she needs him more and more. This acceptance of losers and dysfunctional behavior seems to reveal a deep-seated Christian view of humankind in her lyrics. However, Lana tends, at the same time, to accept a certain naturalistic cynicism, especially on the animalistic side of love, but at the same time, her ideals are Platonic.

The most interesting part of Lana's representation of desire is its repetitive nature. There is an ongoing quest for liberation and unity. It never happens, and can never happen, because even if one initially looks for everlasting love, desire leads to desire for obstacles. Her texts reveal the enormity of subjectivity in love, even in the most unfavorable conditions, and in that way, she goes a step further, dissolving the classical image of love turning to hate when not met. Instead, love becomes an ongoing repetition, creating a desire so strong that one finally yearns for failure. Even if Lana sees love as a subject–subject relation, a triangular structure evolves, where the obstacle becomes desire itself, and there is no way to preserve the exclusive unity between the two lovers. Probably a third party, which she so seldom reveals in her lyrics, is the main reason for the continually ongoing failings and, ultimately, creates a desire for failure, thereby letting desire for obstacles triumph. One could say that by hiding the effect of the third person, the myth surrounding love is born. From this very common experience of love arise songs so beautiful and well composed, in their sad and tragic manner, that Lana herself has become that desired cultural icon she so often sings about in her songs.

Notes

Chapter 1. The Nature of Desire

1. Jean-Michel Oughhourlian, *The Genesis of Desire* (East Lansing: Michigan State University Press, 2010), 88–95.

2. René Girard, *Violence and the Sacred*, 5th ed. (Baltimore: Johns Hopkins University Press, 1986), 147.

3. Ibid., 146 and 145, respectively.

4. Eugene Webb, *Philosophers of Consciousness: Polanyi, Lonergan, Voegelin, Ricoeur, Girard, Kierkegaard* (Seattle: University of Washington Press, 1988), 184.

5. "The dynamism of mimetic desire has always been oriented towards death and madness." See René Girard, *Things Hidden since the Foundation of the World* (London: Athlone Press, 1987), 414. "Mimetic desire thinks that it always chooses the most life-affirming path, whereas

in actuality it turns increasingly towards the obstacle—towards sterility and death." Ibid., 415.

6. See ibid., 162, 322, 416–31; James Williams, ed., *The Girard Reader* (New York: Crossroad, 1996), 161, 198–99, 215–16; René Girard, *I See Satan Fall Like Lightning* (New York: Orbis Books, 2001), 16.

7. Girard, *I See Satan Fall Like Lightning*, 14.

8. A similar development of desire is outlined by Robert Hamerton-Kelly when he claims that it begins by wishing to be like the rival, then wishes to conquer the rival (envy), and finally to destroy the rival. Robert G. Hamerton-Kelly, *The Gospel and the Sacred* (Minneapolis: Fortress, 1994), 134.

9. "Desire can be defined as a process of mimesis involving undifferentiation; it is akin to the process of deepening conflict that issues in the mechanism of reunification through the victim." Girard, *Things Hidden*, 287.

10. James Alison, *The Joy of Being Wrong: Original Sin through Easter Eyes* (New York: Crossroad, 1998), 14.

11. Girard, *Things Hidden*, 294.

12. Ibid., 283.

13. Ibid., 288.

14. Ibid., 285.

15. Ibid., 288.

Chapter 2. Desire in *Madame Bovary*

1. Victor Brombert, *The Novels of Flaubert* (Princeton, NJ: Princeton University Press, 1966), 65–6.

2. Leo Bersani, "Flaubert and Emma Bovary: The Hazards of Literary Fusion," in Bloom, *Flaubert's Madame Bovary*, 28.

3. Corrado Biazzo Curry, *Description and Meaning in Three Novels by Gustave Flaubert* (New York: Peter Lang, 1997), 35.

4. Ibid., 19–31.

5. Tony Tanner, *Adultery in the Novel* (Baltimore: Johns Hopkins University Press, 1979), 320.

6. Hazel Barnes, *Sartre & Flaubert* (Chicago: The University of Chicago Press, 1981), 381.

7. Brombert, *The Novels of Flaubert*, 55.

8. Gustave Flaubert, *Madame Bovary*, trans. Margaret Mauldon (Oxford: Oxford University Press, 2008), 91.

9. Ibid., 79.

10. Ibid., 63–64.

11. Brombert, *The Novels of Flaubert*, 62.

12. Flaubert, *Madame Bovary*, 64–66.

13. Ibid., 33.

14. Ibid.

15. See Brombert, *The Novels of Flaubert*, 54.

16. Flaubert, *Madame Bovary*, 34.

17. Stirling Haig, "The Madame Bovary Blues," in *The Madame Bovary Blues: The Pursuit of Illusion in Nineteenth-Century French Fiction* (Baton Rouge: Louisiana State University Press, 1987), 83.

18. Flaubert, *Madame Bovary*, 36–37.

19. Ibid., 37.

20. Ibid., 22.

21. Ibid., 18.

22. Ibid., 23.

23. Mary Orr, *Madame Bovary: Representations of the Masculine*, Romanticism and After in France 3 (Bern: Peter Lang, 1999), 31–34.

24. Flaubert, *Madame Bovary*, 41.

25. Ibid., 23.

26. Ibid., 23–24.

27. See Henri Peyre, *What Is Romanticism?* (Tuscaloosa: Alabama University Press, 1977).

28. Ibid., 24.

29. Ibid., 18–19, 73.

30. Ibid., 77 ff.

31. Ibid., 89.

32. Flaubert, *Madame Bovary*, 75.

33. Ibid., 34, 36–37. This love, however, refers to things she has never seen.

34. Peyre, *What Is Romanticism?*, 109–27.

35. Ibid., 104.

36. Ibid., 98–108.

37. Ibid., 125–27.

38. Denis de Rougemont, *Love in the Western World* (New York: Harper & Row, 1974), 38 ff.

39. Ibid., 260.

40. Ibid., 267–68.

41. Ibid., 276.

42. Flaubert, *Madame Bovary*, 199.

43. Ibid., 55.

44. Ibid., 57–61.

45. Ibid., 81.

46. Ibid., 50, 54.

47. Ibid., 55.

48. Orr, *Madame Bovary*, 193–94.

49. Ibid., 170.

50. De Rougemont, *Love in the Western World*, 61.

51. Ibid., 112.

52. Ibid., 71.

53. Ibid., 135.

54. Ibid., 166.

55. Flaubert, *Madame Bovary*, 34.

56. Ibid., 52.

57. Ibid., 112–13.

58. See Dominick La Capra, *"Madame Bovary" on Trial* (Ithaca: Cornell University Press, 1986), 30–52.

59. De Rougemont is mentioned in René Girard, *Deceit, Desire, and the Novel: Self and Other in Literary Structure*, trans. Yvonne Freccero (Baltimore: Johns Hopkins University Press) on pages 48, 108, 165, 177–79, 192, 226, 285, 287.

60. Girard, *Deceit, Desire, and the Novel*, 226.

61. Ibid., 287.

62. Ibid., 177–78.

63. Ibid., chap. 1.

64. Ibid.

65. Ibid., 15.

66. Michal Peled Ginsburg, *Flaubert Writing* (Stanford: Stanford University Press, 1986), 84 and 106.

68. Ibid., 88–89.

69. Ibid., 96–97.

70. Ibid., 90–91.

71. Ibid., 94–98.

72. Ibid., 96–97.

73. Ibid., 97.

74. Ibid., 210.

75. Ibid., 216–17.

76. Ibid., 217.

77. Ibid., 123.

78. Ibid., 116.

79. Ibid., 126–33.

80. De Rougemont, *Love in the Western World*, 186.

81. Ibid., 237.

82. Flaubert, *Madame Bovary*, 116.

83. Ibid., part 2, chap. 8.

84. Ibid., 145.

85. Ibid., 304 and 309.

86. Ibid., 310–11.

87. Ibid., 311.

88. Ibid., 252.

89. Ibid.

90. Ibid., 138 and 311.

91. Ibid., 133–34.

92. Barnes, *Sartre & Flaubert*, 379.

93. See Orr, *Madame Bovary*, 212.

94. Geoffrey Wall, *Flaubert: A Life* (London: Faber and Faber, 2001), chap. 17 ("The Pangs of Art").

95. Flaubert, *Madame Bovary*, 289. See also Tanner, *Adultery in the Novel*, 341.

Chapter 3. Proustian Desire

1. Germaine Brée, *The World of Marcel Proust* (Boston: Houghton Mifflin, 1966), 65.

2. Marcel Proust, *In Search of Lost Time*, trans. C. K. Scott

Moncrieff and Terence Kilmartin (London: Vintage, 1996), 6:445–51.

3. René Girard, *Deceit, Desire, and the Novel: Self and Other in Literary Structure*, trans. Yvonne Freccero (Baltimore: Johns Hopkins University Press, 1965), 213–14.

4. Roger Shattuck interprets this break of routine as a symbol of Combray life falling apart. See Roger Shattuck, *Proust's Way* (New York: W. W. Norton, 2000), 28.

5. Proust, *In Search of Lost Time*, 1:127–28.

6. Ibid., 1:127.

7. Ibid., 1:81–82.

8. Ibid., 1:79.

9. Ibid., 1:141–43, 148–58.

10. Ibid., 1:155–58.

11. Ibid., 1:41.

12. Ibid., 1:162.

13. Ibid., 1:162–73.

14. René Girard, *Things Hidden since the Foundation of the World* (London: Athlone Press, 1987), 68.

15. Proust, *In Search of Lost Time*, 1:27–39.

16. Ibid., 1:130.

17. Girard, *Deceit, Desire, and the Novel*, 197.

18. Ibid., 213–14.

19. Proust, *In Search of Lost Time*, 1:17.

20. Ibid., 1:497.

21. Ibid.

22. Ibid., 1:498.

23. Ibid., 1:501.

24. Ibid., 2:72.

25. Ibid., 2:73–74.

26. Ibid., 2:76.

27. Girard, *Deceit, Desire, and the Novel*, 34.

28. Proust, *In Search of Lost Time*, 1:493.

29. Ibid., 1:495.

30. Ibid., 1:481, 1:495.

31. Ibid., 1:495.

32. Ibid., 1:490–91.

33. Ibid., 1:496.

34. Ibid.

35. Ibid., 1:267–70.

36. Ibid., 1:460.

37. Ibid., 1:450–53.

38. Ibid., 1:452–53.

39. Girard, *Things Hidden*, 304.

40. Ibid., 301.

41. Girard, *Deceit, Desire, and the Novel*, 27–28.

42. Ibid., 34; Girard, *Things Hidden*, 397.

43. Girard, *Deceit, Desire, and the Novel*, 34.

44. Ibid., 38.

45. Girard, *Things Hidden*, 397.

46. Proust, *In Search of Lost Time*, 6:68.

47. Jean-Pierre Dupuy, *La jalousie: Une géométrie du désir* (Paris: Seuil, 2016), 34.

48. See chap. 4, "Le enfer proustienne," in Dupuy, *La jalousie*.

49. Ibid., 29–43.

50. Nicolas Grimaldi, *Proust, les horreurs de l'amour* (Paris: Presses Universitaires de France, 2008), 168.

51. Ibid., 169.

52. Ibid., 167.

53. Ibid.

54. Ibid., 171.

55. Ibid., 167.

56. Proust, *In Search of Lost Time*, 2:61.

57. See Henri Peyre, "The Legacy of Proust," in *Proust: A Collection of Critical Essays*, ed. René Girard (Upper Saddle, NJ.: Prentice Hall, 1962), 30–31.

58. Proust, *In Search of Lost Time*, 1:268–70.

59. Ibid., 2:11.

60. Girard, *Deceit, Desire, and the Novel*, 238.

61. Ibid.

62. Samuel Beckett, *Proust* (London: Chatto & Windus, 1931), 7.

63. Girard, *Deceit, Desire, and the Novel*, 80.

64. Ibid., 34.

65. Ibid., 81.

66. Pericles Lewis, *Religious Experience and the Modernist Novel* (Cambridge: Cambridge University Press, 2010), 101.

67. This claim is first made in *Deceit, Desire, and the Novel* and is further elaborated in *Things Hidden* under the title "Proust's Conversion," 393–98.

68. Girard, *Proust: A Collection of Critical Essays*, 11.

69. Proust, *In Search of Lost Time*, 6:446.

70. Interpreting desire will always be dependent on attitude

and biography. The rather dogmatic skepticism of the second half of the twentieth century toward regarding biographical fact as useful in understanding works of art can be seen as a desire to obliterate mimesis in literary interpretation. Instead, mimesis is replaced by ideas, which can be seen as an antimimetic strategy in order to hide the effects of desire. Preoccupation with ideas can be seen, in certain instances, as a way of turning desire into the decisive factor by hiding or omitting its presence. Certain methods of interpretation can be seen as hostility toward using biographical facts and therefore blocking insights into mimetic and/or interdividual desire. Both New Criticism and structuralism have been relatively dismissive of using biography to understand literary texts, while deconstructionism, even if it does not have such a dogmatic dismissal of biography, does not seem keen to use biography as a means to understand novelistic works. There seems, on the whole, to have been a clear antimimetic tendency in nineteenth- and twentieth-century humanistic thought. In this respect coming to grips with desire and how it works has mostly been confined to areas outside science, even to areas outside art and literature. From this point of view Freud's attempt to locate desire, for example in *Zur Einführung des Narzissmus*, must be regarded as a major breakthrough in humanistic science. The fallacy, however, in biographical analysis is its tendency to establish a naïve correspondence between life and art, a tendency that can easily lead to interpreting Proust as identical with both the narrator and the main character (Marcel). This, however, is not only due to a simplistic projection of life into art, but also to the very, very thin veil Proust creates between himself and Marcel. From the perspective of biographical symmetry, it is both possible and legitimate to read *In Search of Lost Time* as a fictionalized autobiography. This symmetry is the fruit of Proust's imitative reconstruction of his past.

71. Proust, *In Search of Lost Time*, 6:446.

72. Ibid. 3:180–85.

73. Shattuck, *Proust's Way*, 39–40.

74. Marcel Proust, *Jean Santeuil*, trans. Gerard Hopkins (London: Panther, 1966), 44.

75. Ibid., 406–10.

76. Beckett, *Proust*, 51–59.

77. Ibid., 61.

78. Ibid., 61–62.

79. In some ways one can see Beckett starting off from where Proust ended: from the point where desires have stripped the characters bare, and there is only baseness, weakness, and conflict left (to write about).

80. Proust, *In Search of Lost Time*, 6:202.

81. Ibid., 6:216.

82. Ibid, 6:202.

83. Ibid.

84. Ibid., 6:254.

85. Ibid., 6:253.

86. Ibid., 6:255.

87. Ibid.

88. Ibid., 6:236.

89. Ibid., 6:255.

90. Ibid., 6:253 and 250.

91. Ibid., 6:235–55.

92. Ibid., 6:321–25.

93. Ibid., 6:399.

94. There is something carnivalesque about the final social gathering at the Guermantes as the aristocrats who before have been considered as the elite are now losing prestige, while people from the lower classes, like Bloch and Rachel, are now the people who are ascending toward the top of the hierarchy. The rather ironic way Proust describes this tendency of destabilizing power reveals a slight conservative streak in Proust's personality.

Chapter 4. Desire in *The Great Gatsby*

1. Nicolas Tredell, *Fitzgerald's "The Great Gatsby"* (New York: Continuum, 2009), 10.

2. James C. Howell, "History of Street Gangs in the United States 4", National Gang Center Bulletin, May 2010, 6.

3. Robert Ornstein, "Scott Fitzgerald's Fable of East and West," *College English*, Vol. 18, No. 3 (Dec., 1956), 55.

4. James E. Miller Jr., "Boats against the Current," in Lockridge, *Twentieth-Century Interpretations of "The Great Gatsby,"* 53.

5. Gunhild Enemo, "'Born Back Ceaselessly into the Past': A Reading of F. Scott Fitzgerald's *The Great Gatsby*" (master's

thesis, Trondheim, Norges teknisk-naturvitenskapelige universitet, 2006), 32.

6. F. Scott Fitzgerald, *The Great Gatsby* (London: Penguin, 2000), 9.

7. Ibid., 158.

8. Lockridge, *Twentieth-Century Interpretations of "The Great Gatsby,"* 10.

9. Fitzgerald, *The Great Gatsby*, 8.

10. Tredell, *Fitzgerald's "The Great Gatsby,"* 19.

11. Gary J. Scrimgeour, "Against *The Great Gatsby*," *Criticism*, Vol. 8, No. 1 (Winter 1966), 73.

12. Ibid., 80.

13. Fitzgerald, *The Great Gatsby*, 58.

14. Ibid., 82–85.

15. Ibid., 171.

16. Tredell, *Fitzgerald's "The Great Gatsby,"* 40–41.

17. Fitzgerald, *The Great Gatsby*, 171.

18. Robert Emmet Long, *The Achieving of "The Great Gatsby": F. Scott Fitzgerald, 1920–1925* (London: Associated University Presses, 1979), 180–81.

19. Tredell, *Fitzgerald's "The Great Gatsby,"* 75.

20. André le Vot, *F. Scott Fitzgerald: A Biography* (New York: Warner Books, 1983), 48–51.

21. Ibid., 48–49.

22. Roger Lewis, "Money, Love, and Aspiration in *The Great Gatsby*," in *New Essays on "The Great Gatsby*," ed. Matthew Bruccoli (Cambridge: Cambridge University Press, 1985), 43. See also Roger Lathbury, "Money, Love, and Aspiration in *The Great Gatsby*," in *Jay Gatsby*, ed. Harold Bloom, Bloom's Major Literary Characters (New York: Chelsea House, 2004), 71.

23. Fitzgerald admitted "The Sensible Thing" was based on him and Zelda, on Zelda breaking up with him and, later, the marriage issue. *The Letters of F. Scott Fitzgerald* (New York: Charles Scribner's Sons, 1963), 189.

24. See W. Lloyd Warner, Marcha Meeker, and Kenneth Eells, "What Social Class Is in America," in *Social Class and Stratification: Classic Statements and Theoretical Debates*, ed. Rhonda F. Levine (Lanham, MD: Rowman & Littlefield, 2006), 74.

25. Fitzgerald, *The Great Gatsby*, 103.

26. Ibid., 115.

27. F. H. Langham, "Style and Shape in *The Great Gatsby*," in Donaldson, *Critical Essays on F. Scott Fitzgerald's "The Great Gatsby*," 47.

28. Lathbury, "Money, Love, and Aspiration in *The Great Gatsby*," 73.

29. Fitzgerald, *The Great Gatsby*, 120–29.

30. Ibid., 139.

31. Ibid., 170.

32. F. Scott Fitzgerald, "The Rich Boy," in *The Collected Short Stories of F. Scott Fitzgerald* (London: Penguin, 1986), 110.

33. Lockridge, *Twentieth-Century Interpretations of "The Great Gatsby*," 13.

34. Ibid., 3.

35. Scrimgeour, "Against *The Great Gatsby*," 73.

36. Le Vot, *F. Scott Fitzgerald*, 13.

37. Fitzgerald, *The Great Gatsby*, 95.

38. Tredell, *Fitzgerald's "The Great Gatsby*," 81–82.

39. Miller, "Boats against the Current," 48.

40. Ibid., 52.

41. Giles Mitchell, "Gatsby Is a Pathological Narcissist," in *Readings on "The Great Gatsby*," ed. Katie de Koster (San

Diego: Greenham Press, 1998), 62.

42. Fitzgerald, *The Great Gatsby*, 20.

43. Ibid., 101.

44. Tredell, *Fitzgerald's "The Great Gatsby,"* 35.

45. Thomas A. Hanzo, "The Theme and the Narrator of *The Great Gatsby*," in Lockridge, *Twentieth-Century Interpretations of "The Great Gatsby,"* 66–68.

46. Thomas J. Cousineau, "The Great Gatsby: Romance or Holocaust?," *Contagion* 8 (2001): 22–28.

47. Stephen L. Gardner, "Democracy and Desire in *The Great Gatsby*," in *Passions in Economy, Politics and the Media*, ed. Wolfgang Palaver and Petra Steinmar-Pösel (Vienna: Lit Verlag, 2005), 281–83.

48. Richard Lehan, "Inventing Gatsby," in Bloom, *Jay Gatsby*, 89–90.

49. F. Scott Fitzgerald, *The Beautiful and Damned* (New York: Scribner's, 1950), 255.

50. Fitzgerald, *The Great Gatsby*, 18. Miller, "Boats against the Current," 31.

51. Tredell, *Fitzgerald's "The Great Gatsby,"* 44.

52. Ibid., 47.

53. Ibid., 86.

54. Ibid., 36.

55. Ibid.

56 Harold Bloom, introduction to *Jay Gatsby*, 4.

57. Hanzo, "The Theme and the Narrator of The Great Gatsby," 64.

58. Careless driving represents a strain of irresponsibility deep in the whole of society. See Langham, "Style and Shape in *The Great Gatsby*," 51.

59. See Scrimgeour, "Against *The Great Gatsby*," 79.

60. Ibid., 75.

61. Langham, "Style and Shape in *The Great Gatsby*."

62. Fitzgerald, *The Great Gatsby*, 95.

63. Tredell, *Fitzgerald's "The Great Gatsby,"* 21.

64. Fitzgerald, *The Great Gatsby*, 107.

65. Ibid., 89.

66. Miller, "Boats against the Current," 39.

67. Fitzgerald, *The Great Gatsby*, 111.

68. Ibid., 106.

69. Irenaeus, *Adversus Haereses* 1.6.2–3, in Hans Jonas, *The Gnostic Religion* (Boston: Beacon Press, 1963), 270–71.

70. David L. Minter, "Dream, Design and Interpretation in *The Great Gatsby*," in Lockridge, *Twentieth-Century Interpretations of "The Great Gatsby*," 87.

71. Fitzgerald, *The Great Gatsby*, 42.

72. Ibid., 153.

73. Jonas, *The Gnostic Religion*, 337.

74. Fitzgerald, *The Great Gatsby*, 85.

75. Ibid., 150.

Chapter 5. Desire in *Death of a Salesman*

1. Jim Cullen, *The American Dream: A Short History of an Idea That Shaped a Nation* (New York: Oxford University Press, 2003), 8.

2. Ibid., 177–78.

3. Arthur Miller, *Death of a Salesman* (London: Penguin, 2000), 40.

4. Brian Parker, "Point of View in Arthur Miller's *Death of a Salesman*," in *Arthur Miller: A Collection of Critical Essays*, ed. Robert W. Corrigan, Twentieth Century Views (Englewood Cliffs, NJ.: Prentice-Hall, 1969), 102.

5. Harold Bloom, ed., *Arthur Miller's Death of a Salesman*

(New York: Chelsea House, 2004), 8.

6. Miller, *Death of a Salesman*, 53.

7. Ibid., 11.

8. Ibid., 54.

9. Ibid., 23.

10. Ibid., 54.

11. Matthew C. Roudané, "*Death of a Salesman* and the Poetics of Arthur Miller," in *The Cambridge Companion to Arthur Miller*, ed. Christopher Bigsy, 2nd ed. (Cambridge: Cambridge University Press, 2010), 72.

12. Cullen, *The American Dream*, 182.

13. Miller, *Death of a Salesman*, 11.

14. Ibid., 43.

15. Ibid., 47.

16. Ibid., 53.

17. Ibid., 95.

18. Ronald Hayman, *Arthur Miller*, Contemporary Playwrights (London: Heineman, 1977), 30.

19. Miller, *Death of a Salesman*, 48.

20. Ibid.

21. T. S. Eliot, *The Waste Land*, in T. S. Eliot, *Collected Poems*,

1909–1962 (London: Faber & Faber, 1983), 61–86.

22. Miller, *Death of a Salesman*, 40.

23. Eliot, *The Waste Land*, lines 1–2.

24. Miller, *Death of a Salesman*, 12.

25. Eliot, *The Waste Land*, lines 69–76.

26. Ibid., lines 208–14.

27. Ibid., lines 233–34.

28. Ibid., line 103.

29. Miller, *Death of a Salesman*, 96.

Chapter 6. Desire in Lana Del Rey

1. For Lana Del Rey's lyrics, see http://search.azlyrics.com/
   search.php?q=lana+del+rey.

2. Jim Cullen, *The American Dream: A Short History of an
   Idea That Shaped a Nation* (New York: Oxford University
   Press, 2003), 8.

3. René Girard, *I See Satan Fall like Lightning* (New York:
   Orbis Books, 2001), 11.

4. Kayla Simpson, *Lana Del Rey* (Amazon: Great Britain,
   Kayla Simpson, 2015).

5. Irenaeus, *Adversus Haereses* 1.6.2–3, in Hans Jonas, *The Gnostic Religion* (Boston: Beacon Press, 1963), 270–71.

6. For "Scandalon" in René Girard's work, see e.g., *Things Hidden since the Foundation of the World* (London: Athlone Press, 1987), 162, 322, 416–31.

7. Ibid., 416.

8. Ibid.

9. Ibid., 426.

10. Ibid., 430.

11. Georg Wilhelm Friedrich Hegel, *Phenomenology of the Spirit* (Oxford: Oxford University Press, 1977), 166.

12. Allen Wood, *Hegel's Ethical Thought* (Cambridge: Cambridge University Press, 1990), 84.

13. René Girard, *Deceit, Desire, and the Novel: Self and Other in Literary Structure*, trans. Yvonne Freccero (Baltimore: Johns Hopkins University Press, 1965).

14. Hegel, *Phenomenology of the Spirit*, 175.

15. Ibid.

16. Ibid., 175–76.

17. Ibid., 182.

18. Ibid., 187.

19. Philippe Lacoue-Labarthe, *Typography: Mimesis, Philosophy, Politics* (Cambridge, MA: Harvard University Press, 1989), 127.

20. Hegel, *Phenomenology of the Spirit*, 190.

21. Kojève, however, interprets the master's role toward the slave as a catalyst toward freedom. See Alexandre Kojève, *Introduction to the Reading of Hegel: Lectures on the Phenomenology of the Spirit* (Ithaca: Cornell University Press, 1980), 7.

22. Paul Virilio, *Speed and Politics: An Essay on Dromology* (New York: Semiotext(e), 1977).

23. *Lana Del Rey: The Greatest Story Never Told* (Iconic Pictures, 2013).

24. Denis de Rougemont, *Love in the Western World* (New York: Harper & Row, 1974), 260.

25. Ibid., 267–68.

26. Ibid., 38 ff.

27. Ibid., 263–64.

28. Ibid., 260–63, 268.

29. Girard, *Deceit, Desire, and the Novel*, 287.

30. De Rougemont, *Love in the Western World*, 313.

31. Ibid., 316.

32. Ibid., 186.

Bibliography

Alison, James. *The Joy of Being Wrong: Original Sin through Easter Eyes*. New York: Crossroad, 1998.

Barnes, Hazel. "The Biographer as Literary Critic: Sartre's Flaubert and Madame Bovary." In Bloom, *Flaubert's Madame Bovary*.

Beckett, Samuel. *Proust*. London: Chatto & Windus, 1931.

Bersani, Leo. "Flaubert and Emma Bovary: The Hazards of Literary Fusion." In Bloom, *Flaubert's Madame Bovary*.

Bigsy, Christopher, ed. *The Cambridge Companion to Arthur Miller*, 2nd ed. Cambridge: Cambridge University Press, 2010.

Bloom, Harold, ed. *Arthur Miller's Death of a Salesman*. New York: Chelsea House, 2004.

——— , ed. *Flaubert's Madame Bovary*. Modern Critical

Interpretations. Philadelphia: Chelsea House, 1988.

———, ed. *Jay Gatsby*. Bloom's Major Literary Characters. New York: Chelsea House, 2004.

Brée, Germaine. *The World of Marcel Proust*. Boston: Houghton Mifflin, 1966.

Brombert, Victor. "The Tragedy of Dreams." In Bloom, *Flaubert's Madame Bovary*.

Cousineau, Thomas J. "*The Great Gatsby*: Romance or Holocaust?" *Contagion* 8 (2001): 21–38.

Cullen, Jim. *The American Dream: A Short History of an Idea That Shaped a Nation*. New York: Oxford University Press, 2003.

Curry, Corrado Biazzo. *Description and Meaning in Three Novels by Gustave Flaubert*. New York: Peter Lang, 1997.

de Rougemont, Denis. *Love in the Western World*. New York: Harper & Row, 1974.

Donaldson, Scott. "The Life of F. Scott Fitzgerald." In *Critical Essays on F. Scott Fitzgerald's "The Great Gatsby,"* edited by Scott Donaldson. Boston: G. K. Hall, 1984.

Dupuy, Jean-Pierre. *La jalousie: Une géométrie du désir*. Paris: Seuil, 2016.

Enemo, Gunhild. "'Born Back Ceaselessly into the Past': A Reading of F. Scott Fitzgerald's *The Great Gatsby*." Master's thesis, Trondheim, Norges teknisk-naturvitenskapelige universitet, 2006.

Eliot, T. S. *Collected Poems, 1909–1962*. London: Faber & Faber, 1983.

Emmet Long, Robert. *The Achieving of "The Great Gatsby": F. Scott Fitzgerald, 1920–1925*. London: Associated University Presses, 1979.

Fitzgerald, F. Scott. *The Beautiful and Damned*. New York: Scribner's, 1950.

———. *The Collected Short Stories of F. Scott Fitzgerald*. London: Penguin, 1986.

———. *The Great Gatsby*. Boston: G. K. Hall, 1984.

———. *The Great Gatsby*. London: Penguin, 2000.

———. *The Letters of F. Scott Fitzgerald*. New York: Charles Scribner's Sons, 1963.

———. *This Side of Paradise*. London: Penguin, 1920.

Flaubert, Gustave. *Madame Bovary*. Translated by Margaret Mauldon. Oxford: Oxford University Press, 2008.

Gardner, Stephen L. "Democracy and Desire in *The Great*

Gatsby." In *Passions in Economy, Politics and the Media*, edited by Wolfgang Palaver and Petra Steinmar-Pösel. Vienna: Lit Verlag, 2005.

Ginsburg, Michael Peled. "Narrative Strategies in *Madame Bovary*." In Bloom, *Flaubert's Madame Bovary*.

Girard, René. *Deceit, Desire, and the Novel: Self and Other in Literary Structure*. Translated by Yvonne Freccero. Baltimore: Johns Hopkins University Press, 1965.

———. *Des Choses cachées depuis la fondation du monde: Recherches avec Jean-Michel Oughourlian et Guy Lefort*. Paris: Grasset, 1978.

———. *The Girard Reader*. Edited by James Williams. New York: Crossroad, 1996.

———. *I See Satan Fall Like Lightning*. New York: Orbis Books, 2001.

———. *Mensonge romantique et vérité romanesque*. Paris: Grasset, 1961.

———, ed. *Proust: A Collection of Critical Essays*. Englewood Cliffs, NJ: Prentice-Hall, 1962.

———. *Quand ces choses commenceront: Entretiens avec Michel Treguer*. Paris: Arlèa, 1994.

———. *The Scapegoat*. Baltimore: Johns Hopkins University Press, 1986.

———. *Things Hidden since the Foundation of the World*. London: Athlone Press, 1987.

———. *Violence and the Sacred*. 5th ed. Baltimore: Johns Hopkins University Press, 1986.

———. *La Violence et le sacré*. Paris: Grasset, 1972.

Grimaldi, Nicolas. *Proust, les horreurs de l'amour*. Paris: Presses Universitaires de France, 2008.

Haig, Stirling. *The Madame Bovary Blues: The Pursuit of Illusion in Nineteenth-Century French Fiction*. Baton Rouge: Louisiana State University Press, 1987.

Hamerton-Kelly, Robert G. *The Gospel and the Sacred*. Minneapolis: Fortress, 1994.

Hanzo, Thomas A. "The Theme and the Narrator of *The Great Gatsby*." In *Twentieth-Century Interpretations of "The Great Gatsby": A Collection of Critical Essays*, edited by Ernest H. Lockridge. Englewood Cliffs, NJ: Prentice-Hall, 1968.

Hayman, Ronald. *Arthur Miller*. Contemporary Playwrights. London: Heineman, 1977.

Hegel, Georg Wilhelm Friedrich. *Phenomenology of the Spirit*.

Oxford: Oxford University Press, 1977.

Howell, James C. "History of Street Gangs in the United States 4." National Gang Center Bulletin, May 2010.

Irenaeus. *Adversus Haereses* I. 6.2–3. In Hans Jonas, *The Gnostic Religion*. Boston: Beacon Press, 1963.

Jonas, Hans. *The Gnostic Religion*. Boston: Beacon Press, 1963.

Kojève, Alexandre. *Introduction to the Reading of Hegel: Lectures on the Phenomenology of the Spirit*. Ithaca: Cornell University Press, 1980.

La Capra, Dominick. "The Trial." In Bloom, *Flaubert's Madame Bovary*.

Lacoue-Labarthe, Philippe. *Typography: Mimesis, Philosophy, Politics*. Cambridge, MA: Harvard University Press, 1989.

Lana Del Rey: The Greatest Story Never Told. Iconic Pictures, 2013.

Langham, F. H. "Style and Shape in *The Great Gatsby*." In *Critical Essays on F. Scott Fitzgerald's "The Great Gatsby,"* edited by Scott Donaldson. Boston: G. K. Hall, 1984.

Lathbury, Roger. "Money, Love, and Aspiration in *The Great Gatsby*." In Bloom, *Jay Gatsby*.

Lehan, Richard. "Inventing Gatsby." In Bloom, *Jay Gatsby*.

Lewis, Pericles. *Religious Experience and the Modernist Novel.* Cambridge: Cambridge University Press, 2010.

Lewis, Roger. "Money, Love, and Aspiration in *The Great Gatsby.*" In *New Essays on "The Great Gatsby,"* edited by Matthew Bruccoli. Cambridge: Cambridge University Press, 1985.

Lockridge, Ernest H., ed. *Twentieth-Century Interpretations of "The Great Gatsby": A Collection of Critical Essays.* Englewood Cliffs, NJ: Prentice-Hall, 1968.

Miller, Arthur. *Death of a Salesman.* London: Penguin, 2000.

Miller, James E., Jr. "Boats against the Current." In *Twentieth-Century Interpretations of "The Great Gatsby": A Collection of Critical Essays*, edited by Ernest H. Lockridge. Englewood Cliffs, NJ: Prentice-Hall, 1968.

Minter, David L. "Dream, Design and Interpretation in *The Great Gatsby.*" In *Twentieth-Century Interpretations of "The Great Gatsby": A Collection of Critical Essays*, edited by Ernest H. Lockridge. Englewood Cliffs, NJ: Prentice-Hall, 1968.

Mitchell, Giles. "Gatsby Is a Pathological Narcissist." In *Readings on "The Great Gatsby,"* edited by Katie de Koster. San

Diego: Greenham Press, 1998.

Ornstein, Robert. "Scott Fitzgerald's Fable of East and West." In
    Twentieth-Century Interpretations of "The Great Gatsby": A
    Collection of Critical Essays, edited by Ernest H. Lockridge.
    Englewood Cliffs, NJ: Prentice-Hall, 1968.

Orr, Mary. *Madame Bovary: Representations of the Masculine.*
    Romanticism and After in France 3. Bern: Peter Lang,
    1999.

Oughhourlian, Jean-Michel. *The Genesis of Desire*. East Lansing:
    Michigan State University Press, 2010.

Parker, Brian. "Point of View in Arthur Miller's *Death of a*
    Salesman." In *Arthur Miller: A Collection of Critical Essays*,
    edited by Robert W. Corrigan, Twentieth Century Views.
    Englewood Cliffs, NJ: Prentice-Hall, 1969.

Peyre, Henri. "The Legacy of Proust." In *Proust: A Collection of*
    Critical Essays, edited by René Girard. Upper Saddle, NJ:
    Prentice Hall, 1962.

———. *What Is Romanticism?* Tuscaloosa: Alabama University
    Press, 1977.

Proust, Marcel. *In Search of Lost Time*. Translated by C. K. Scott
    Moncrieff and Terence Kilmartin. 6 vols. London: Vintage,

1996.

———. *Jean Santeuil*. Translated by Gerard Hopkins. London: Panther, 1966.

Roudané, Matthew C. "*Death of a Salesman* and the Poetics of Arthur Miller." In *The Cambridge Companion to Arthur Miller*, edited by Christopher Bigsy, 2nd ed. Cambridge: Cambridge University Press, 2010.

Scrimgeour, Gary J. "Against *The Great Gatsby*." In *Twentieth-Century Interpretations of "The Great Gatsby": A Collection of Critical Essays*, edited by Ernest H. Lockridge. Englewood Cliffs, NJ: Prentice-Hall, 1968.

Shattuck, Roger. *Proust's Way*. New York: W. W. Norton, 2000.

Simpson, Kayla. *Lana Del Rey*. Self-published, CreateSpace, 2015.

Tanner, Tony. *Adultery in the Novel*. Baltimore: Johns Hopkins University Press, 1979.

———. "The Morselization of *Emma Bovary*." In Bloom, *Flaubert's Madame Bovary*.

Tredell, Nicolas. *Fitzgerald's "The Great Gatsby."* New York: Continuum, 2009.

Virilio, Paul. *Speed and Politics: An Essay on Dromology*. New

York: Semiotext(e), 1977.

Vot, André le. *F. Scott Fitzgerald: A Biography*. New York: Warner Books, 1983.

Wall, Geoffrey. *Flaubert: A Life*. London: Faber and Faber, 2001.

Warner, W. Lloyd, Marcha Meeker, and Kenneth Eells. "What Social Class Is in America." In *Social Class and Stratification: Classic Statements and Theoretical Debates*, edited by Rhonda F. Levine. Lanham, MD: Rowman & Littlefield, 2006.

Webb, Eugene. *Philosophy of Consciousness: Polanyi, Lonergan, Voegelin, Ricoeur, Girard, Kierkegaard*. Seattle: University of Washington Press, 1988.

Williams, James, ed. *The Girard Reader*. New York: Crossroad, 1996.

Wood, Allen. *Hegel's Ethical Thought*. Cambridge: Cambridge University Press, 1990.